by Richard Lamparski

Lamparski's

Hidden

Hollywood

Where the Stars Lived, Loved, and Died

This book is dedicated to Hollywood's Prince of the Past,

SAMSON DE BRIER

Copyright © 1981 by Richard Lamparski
All rights reserved
including the right of reproduction
in whole or in part in any form
A Fireside Book
Published by Simon and Schuster
A Division of Gulf & Western Corporation
Simon & Schuster Building
Rockefeller Center
1230 Avenue of the Americas
New York, New York 10020

FIRESIDE and colophon are trademarks of Simon & Schuster
Designed by Irving Perkins Associates
Manufactured in the United States of America
Printed and bound by Halliday Lithograph
1   2   3   4   5   6   7   8   9   10

Library of Congress Cataloging in Publication Data

Lamparski, Richard.
    Lamparski's Hidden Hollywood.

    (A Fireside book)
    1. Moving-picture actors and actresses—Homes and
haunts—California—Hollywood.   2. Moving-picture
actors and actresses—California—Hollywood—Biography
—Miscellanea.   3. Hollywood, (Calif.)—Dwellings.
I. Title.   II. Title: Hidden Hollywood.
PN1993.5.U65L3   1981   791.43'028'0922 [B]   81-5352
                                                         AACR2

ISBN 0-671-41885-8

Acknowledgments

The author gratefully acknowledges those who have helped to make this book possible:

Paul Adrian
John Agar
Allied Artists Corp.
Kirk Alyn
Hector Arce
Steven Arnold
Michael Back
Al Bang
Dick Bann
William W. Bann
Mrs. Elaine Barrie-Barrymore
William Bass
Beverly Hills Public Library
Roy Bishop
Bob Board
DeWitt Bodeen
Margaret Bourke
Eddie Brandt's Saturday Matinee
Myron Braum
Maury Bresloff
R. T. Brier
Louise Brooks
Karen Bunde
Frank Buxton
Diana Serra Cary
Bill Chapman
Chapman's Picture Palace

Cinemabilia
Columbia Pictures Corp.
Bruce Cook
Tommy Cooper
Bob Cushman
David Dahl
Bill Dakota
Shelly Davis
Samson DeBrier
Walt Disney Productions
Tim Doherty
Jimmie Duffy III of Hillcrest Motor
    Company, Beverly Hills, California
George Eells
Richard Fletcher
Leslie Flint
Tom Folino
Leatrice Fountain
Janet Gaynor-Gregory
Hal Gefsky
Sheilah Graham
Matthew Monroe Haimsohn
Michael Anthony Haimsohn
Lucille Hardy-Price
Aurand Harris
Doug J. Hart's Back Lot
Michael R. Hawks

Howard W. Hays
Terry Helgesen
Charles Higham
Hillcrest Motor Company of Beverly Hills
David Horii
Herman Hover
Jamie James
Mrs. Buck Jones
Leatrice Joy
Barry Kehoe
Michael Knowles
Don Koll
Jack Larson
Anton La Vey
Aileen Leslie
Charles Lockwood
Jay Loft-Lynn
Mary Loos
Los Angeles Herald-Examiner
Los Angeles Times
Dick Lynch
James W. Mace
Wayne Martin
Mike Marx
Sam Marx
Joe Mass
Byron Matson
Metro-Goldwyn-Mayer Corp.
Don Miller
Montgomery Management Co.
Carlotta Monti
National Screen Service Corp.
Sloan Nibley
Merle Norman Cosmetics Tower of Beauty
Paramount Pictures Corp.
Pearl Parks
Wayne Parks
R. C. Perry
Victor R. Plukas
Mary-Robin Redd

Virginia I. Reidy
Tom Rettig, Sr.
Dorothy Revier
Sarah Richardson
Terry T. Roach and the staff of the Library
    of the Academy of Motion Picture Arts
    and Sciences
Art Ronnie
Lili St. Cyr
Robert B. Satterfield
Donna Schaeffer
Paul Schaeffer
Peter Schaeffer
Richard Schaeffer
Schaeffer Photo Lab
Anne Schlosser and the staff of the Library
    of the American Film Institute
Don Schneider of the Electric Theatre
    Movie Museum
Security Pacific National Bank
Rev. Sue Sikking
Tony Slide
Sons of the Desert
Bill Tangeman
Bob Thomas
Mathew Tombers
Twentieth Century Fox Corp.
United Artists
Universal Pictures Corp.
Jon Virzi
Paul Wallach
John Walsh
Marc Wanamaker of Bison Archives
Warner Bros., Inc.
Manny Weltman
Wide World Photos
Cicci Wilson
Ruth Windfeldt
Sandy Brown Wyeth
D. A. Yallop

Contents

Foreword

"What is Hollywood *really* like?"

I was still in my teens and had been in Hollywood about ten days when I was first asked that question. My cousin Bobby, who had joined the Air Force at the same time I had left home, asked it in the first letter he wrote to me.

Bobby and I had often speculated about Hollywood on our frequent walks to and from the movie theaters in our neighborhood, Detroit's east side. There were seven within a six-block radius of our homes. We went to all of them as often as we were allowed. Bobby and I were Depression kids. "Going to the show" was a real treat.

Since I first came to Hollywood I've lived here off and on for over fourteen years. I've written books about the stars and talked with them on my radio program. I've experienced Hollywood as a "name" and as a nonentity. Two of the things Hollywood is best at are paying attention to those it thinks are "somebody" and ignoring those it considers "nobody." I've been both, yet I am still unable to tell Bobby what this place is really like.

None of the many things that have been written about Hollywood has ever caught it completely. *What Makes Sammy Run?*, *The Bad and the Beautiful* and *The Day of the Locust* are vivid as far as they go. But Hollywood has yet to be captured either in a book or on the screen.

Hollywood has been described as "a series of suburbs in search of a city." Another thing it is called is "a state of mind." My favorite, because I have seen the way it treats people and places it no longer considers to be "box-office," is "the town without a memory."

Actually, there *is* no Hollywood, and there hasn't been since that area was absorbed into the sprawling city of Los Angeles in 1910. You'll find addresses in this book for such areas as Silverlake, Culver City, Beverly Hills, Atwater and Malibu. None of these places is Hollywood in the strict sense, but to me, they all are, because the aura of Hollywood is throughout all of them.

This book will show you what Hollywood looks like. It is a tour of all of the places fans have heard of and a few that only the most dedicated buffs have known about until now. If you visit these places—

9

and most of them still exist—you'll experience another dimension of Hollywood. The book will also tell you about some of the delicious and depressing and depraved and delightful things that have happened here. It will confirm some rumors and shatter some legends. Those are two other things that Hollywood has always been best at—creating illusion and disillusion.

I wish Bobby and his counterparts everywhere an enjoyable, interesting trip through these pages. Much of what you will see was built by the stars but with us—the fans—in mind. They wanted to impress us and to amuse us. They wanted to make us envy them and to fall in love with them. Just as we did when we watched them on the screen. No one appreciates Hollywood more than us, the moviegoers, the fans. Or, as "Norma Desmond" so graciously called us, "Those wonderful people out there in the dark."

Welcome to Hollywood!

—RICHARD LAMPARSKI

Beverly Aadland

Beverly Aadland was a real-life Lolita. She was fifteen years old when she became the traveling companion of Errol Flynn, who was thirty years her senior.

After Flynn died in 1959, Beverly took up with a handsome young man named Billy Stanciu. His friends called him Billy the Kid.

On April 11, 1960, Hollywood police responded to a call and arrived at Beverly's apartment at 1780 North El Cerrito Place. Billy, who Beverly said had been playing Russian roulette, was naked and had been shot in the head. His death was declared a suicide.

Billy "the Kid" Stanciu died on his twenty-first birthday.

Paul Adrian

Abbott & Costello

National Screen Service Corp.

On August 16, 1953, the Internal Revenue Service took Abbott's Backstage, a bar in Sherman Oaks, away from its owner, Bud Abbott, for nonpayment of taxes.

Like Lou Costello, Abbott was a compulsive gambler. Unlike his partner, he was a heavy drinker (Dewar's Scotch and water) as well.

The bar was renamed the Hideout by its new owner, who was once Bud Abbott's bartender. He likes to tell about the Saturday night that Abbott and Costello walked in together:

"The place was filled and there was nowhere for them to sit down.

" 'I thought you owned this joint,' says Costello. 'You invite a friend in here for a drink and you can't even ask him to sit down.'

"That did it. Bud told me to close the place. Now it was just a bit past eleven P.M. on a Saturday night, but everyone there had to finish his drink and leave. Then the two of them sat down at a table and had me serve them a few rounds.

"Bud Abbott was a terrible businessman, but there wasn't a better boss in the world. He had a very big heart. God rest his soul."

Paul Adrian

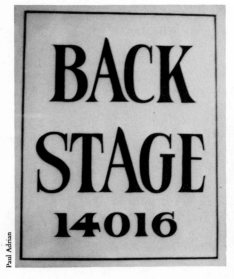

Paul Adrian

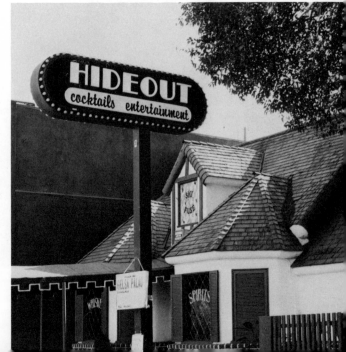

Alfalfa

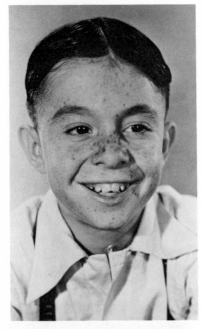

BELOVED FATHER
SON AND BROTHER
CARL "ALFALFA" SWITZER
AUG. 7, 1927   JAN. 21, 1959

Paul Adrian 1979

He was known all over the world as Alfalfa, one of the most popular of *Our Gang* or *Little Rascals,* as the films are now called. But after appearing in fifty-nine of those shorts between 1935 and 1940, Carl Switzer could find very few parts in other movies.

By 1959, Alfalfa was earning his living working as a hunting guide for Roy Rogers and as a part-time bartender.

One day a man who was living with the estranged wife of western star Ray "Crash" Corrigan let Alfalfa take his hunting dog along on a short trip. When the animal disappeared Alfalfa offered a $50 reward, which was promptly claimed.

Alfalfa returned the dog and, explaining what had happened, asked to be reimbursed. The owner did not feel responsible and refused. When the two men got into a fist fight, Alfalfa pulled out a switchblade knife. The other man got his .38 revolver. During the struggle over the gun, Alfalfa was shot dead. The killing was ruled "justifiable homicide."

Another family now lives in the house where Alfalfa was killed: 10400 Columbus Avenue, Mission Hills. The children of the home collect five cents from any neighbor kid who would like to see the bullet hole in the wall, the only sign that remains of the child star's death years ago.

Carl "Alfalfa" Switzer is buried in Hollywood Memorial Park Cemetery, only a few hundred yards from the final resting place of Darla Hood, the sweetheart of *Our Gang,* who is buried in the Abbey of the Psalms.

10400

Paul Adrian 1979

Gwili André

Gwili André was brought to RKO in 1932 by David O. Selznick, who then headed production at that studio. But the woman who was known as "America's most beautiful model" seemed lifeless in all of the ten films she made in Hollywood.

By 1959 her career was long over and her second husband had won custody of her only child. That year the Danish beauty burned to death on February 5, the day after her fifty-second birthday. She left behind some empty whiskey bottles and a box of national magazines featuring her face on the covers. On top of the stack was this publicity still.

"She drank a good deal, poor soul," said a neighbor. "She's found peace at least," commented her landlady. "Something she never knew on this earth."

There is now a parking lot facing the Pacific Ocean where Gwili André's shabby apartment once stood at 2109-B Ocean Front in Venice, California.

Paul Adrian 1980

Fatty Arbuckle

Merle Norman Cosmetics Tower of Beauty

Bison Archives

Roscoe "Fatty" Arbuckle first became a star in the two-reelers he made at the Mack Sennett Keystone studios which were at 1712 Glendale Boulevard in Silverlake. The stage where movies had been made since 1915 is still standing. It was there that Charlie Chaplin and Mabel Normand made their early films. It was also the home of the Keystone Kops.

Arbuckle's McFarlan Cabriolet cost $9,000 in 1923. Still in mint condition, it is on display at the Merle Norman Tower of Beauty in Sylmar, California.

Paul Adrian 1979

By the late twenties Arbuckle had a nightclub, the Plantation Club, in the 10900 block of Washington Boulevard in Culver City.

On opening night, Mabel Normand sent her former co-star a life-size model of himself made of flowers. Her husband, Lew Cody, emceed the show while Tom Mix led the orchestra. Some of the first-nighters were Mary Pickford, Douglas Fairbanks, Sr., Buster Keaton, the three Talmadge sisters, Harry Langdon, Ruth Roland, Bebe Daniels and directors James Cruze and Marshall Nielan.

Bison Archives

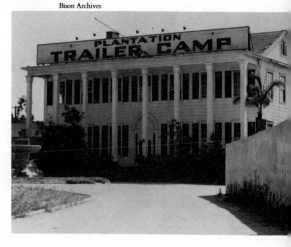

Another night, Al Jolson sang thirty songs in a row. John Barrymore and Jackie Coogan worked together in a comedy routine. Fanny Brice and Leatrice Joy did turns on other evenings. Even mogul Jack Warner was once induced to sing for Fatty's patrons.

After Arbuckle sold the Plantation Club in 1930 it was turned into a trailer park.

Fatty Arbuckle was every bit as popular a screen comedian and director as Charlie Chaplin until he was accused of manslaughter after the death of Virginia Rappe, a bit player in silents. She died after a party held in Arbuckle's suite on the twelfth floor of the St. Francis Hotel in San Francisco on Labor Day, 1921.

The three trials that followed his arrest cost Arbuckle every cent he had. When the third trial ended the jury returned after one minute. Not only was Arbuckle found not guilty, but the jurors apologized to him. They felt he should never have been indicted. The judge concurred.

Fatty Arbuckle bought the Tudor mansion at 649 West Adams Boulevard in Los Angeles shortly before the scandal for $250,000. It had been lived in previously by silent screen vamp Theda Bara. Its front door, which was hand-carved in Spain, cost $15,000, and the chandelier in the dining room held a thousand candles. The garage housed Roscoe's Cadillac, Renault and Rolls-Royce and a $25,000 Pierce Arrow, which was fitted with a bar and toilet.

Arbuckle sold the house to producer Joe Schenck and his wife Norma Talmadge after the third trial to help pay his debts. It was rented sometime later to Greta Garbo. The structure is now the rectory of a Roman Catholic parish.

Virginia Rappe is buried in Hollywood Memorial Park Cemetery. Fatty Arbuckle was cremated after he died in New York City in 1932. In spite of the fact that he was completely exonerated, he died, according to friends, "a broken man."

Paul Adrian 1979

Paul Adrian 19

16

Gene Autry's Melody Ranch

Melody Ranch remains very much the same as it appeared in the Gene Autry movies and TV shows. Located on Oak Creek Canyon Road in Newhall, California, the spread was used also as a locale in the television series *Annie Oakley* and *The Range Rider.*

Melody Ranch is not open to the public.

Paul Adrian 1980

n 1980

Paul Adrian 1980

17

Anne Baxter and John Hodiak

Anne Baxter and John Hodiak seemed very right for each other when they co-starred in *Sunday Dinner for a Soldier* (1944). Two years later, to the delight of their fans, they became husband and wife.

Anne's maternal grandfather's wedding present was the renovation of their house at 8650 Pine Tree Place just off the Sunset Strip. The modernization of a honeymoon house might seem a generous gift for any young couple, but Miss Baxter's grandfather did more than just pay for the reconstruction. He designed and supervised all the work personally. His name was Frank Lloyd Wright.

The home has undergone no major changes since John and Anne divorced in 1953. Hodiak died two years later of a heart attack. Since then the house has been lived in by Frankie Avalon, Fabian and Sir Laurence Olivier.

Its present owner is a Hollywood agent. Not long ago his client and houseguest Lawrence Luckinbill heard Anne Baxter's distinctive voice outside. He looked out the window and saw the star standing in the driveway talking with an acquaintance about her former residence. Luckinbill opened the door and asked if she would like to come inside and look around.

"No, thank you," she replied. "I spent the happiest years of my life in there and I think it's better that it remain a memory to me."

Sandy Brown Wyeth 1979

Louise Beavers

Before Louise Beavers began her career in movies she spent twelve years as the personal maid to silent screen star Leatrice Joy.

Louise Beavers lived within a few minutes' walk of Hattie McDaniel's home, but the two saw very little of each other. Louise was often on the road with Mae West. When she was at home and not making a picture she lived mostly at night.

On the third floor of her home at 2219 Hobart, which is in the part of Los Angeles known as Sugar Hill, the lights burned into the wee, small hours while Louise and her friends played poker. The actress who became famous as Mae West's maid had a husband who waited on her hand and foot whenever she was in residence. He was a professional chef who outdid himself with food and drink at his wife's poker parties.

From time to time the couple

Universal Pictures Corp.

allowed other artists to live in their home as paying guests. One longtime resident was the singer-organist Earl Grant, who occupied the second floor.

Paul Adrian 1979

Wallace Beery

Metro-Goldwyn-Mayer

When Wallace Beery became the first husband of Gloria Swanson in 1916 he was already a "name" but she was almost a nobody. When they divorced three years later Swanson was on the verge of superstardom and he was about to begin a decade of playing mostly villains.

By the early thirties, Beery had become one of MGM's highest-paid stars and was known to millions as the lovable old cuss. As late as 1940 he was still one of those on the *Motion Picture Herald*'s list of the ten most popular movie stars in the world.

When Beery played the ruthless industrialist in Grand Hotel *(1932) he was living in this house. The home at 921 Roxbury Drive in Beverly Hills was almost unchanged in 1980.*

Bison Archives

The Black Dahlia

The press dubbed Elizabeth Short the Black Dahlia because she was seldom seen in anything but all-black dresses and accessories. This photo was taken shortly before she was found murdered in 1947.

On January 15, 1947, the nude body of a young woman was found in a weed-choked vacant lot on South Norton Street between 39th and Coliseum in Los Angeles. She had been cut neatly in half, sliced surgically at the waist. Authorities have never revealed all of the grisly details of the case that is known as the Black Dahlia murder.

Elizabeth Short, the Black Dahlia, moved around a great deal after coming to Hollywood from Hyde Park, Massachusetts. One place she often stayed was the Las Palmas Hotel at 1738 North Las Palmas, just above Hollywood Boulevard.

Elizabeth was called the Black Dahlia because she almost always wore outfits of all black. The twenty-two-year-old was known as a flirt and a tease at places where she used to hang out, such as the Hollywood Playhouse. That little theater stood near the southeast corner of Hollywood Boulevard and Western Avenue, where the Bank of America parking lot is now.

Thirty-three years after the crime the manager of the Hollywood Playhouse said of Elizabeth Short:

"Her clothes weren't the only thing black about that girl. She had a presence that was very unsavory. I couldn't put my finger on exactly what it was but something about her always made me wish she would go away and stay away."

The Black Dahlia murder has never been solved.

When Elizabeth Short was in Hollywood she usually stayed at the Las Palmas Hotel just north of Hollywood Boulevard.

A police mug shot of Elizabeth Short, the Black Dahlia.

C. C. Brown's

C. C. Brown's, the confectioner's, has been a hangout for movie stars since 1929. Many used to walk there after watching their own films just a block away at Grauman's Chinese Theatre. Fans didn't pester them because the real star at Brown's is the famous hot fudge sundae they serve.

When the teenage Judy Garland used to go on a sweets binge, Brown's was where she did it.

One day in 1936 a pretty girl sold William Demarest, who was then an agent, some C. C. Brown's chocolates. Demarest told her she was pretty enough to be in movies. It turned out that was why she had come to Hollywood.

Demarest took the girl with the quiet charm to Paramount Pictures, where a screen test was made. She became Ellen Drew and starred in such films as *Christmas in July* (1940), *My Favorite Spy* (1942) and *Johnny O'Clock* (1947).

Brown's is still at 7007 Hollywood Boulevard, directly across from the Hollywood Roosevelt Hotel.

Some people pass up the hot fudge in favor of the Cinderella Sundae, which Ellen Drew created in 1936.

Burns & Allen

The house that millions of television viewers became so familiar with over the many years on the *Burns and Allen Show* was a set—an exact duplicate of their own home. The single exception was the house number, 320. The home that George and Gracie shared for so many years was at 920 North Maple Drive in Beverly Hills.

George and Gracie raised their adopted children, Sandra and Ronnie, at 920 North Maple Drive.

George Burns and Gracie Allen in 1937 in front of their Beverly Hills home.

Bison Archives

The Café Gala

The Café Gala was opened at 8795 Sunset Boulevard in September 1941 by owner-host John Walsh, an American who had headlined as a singer-pianist in London and Paris during the thirties. Candles provided much of the lighting. The decor was described at the time as "Continental Moderne."

The Gala had a different policy and ambiance from any of the other Hollywood nighteries. The acts that played there were more often than not performers who were not yet known to the general public. Some had small, enthusiastic followings. Others were completely unknown. Celebrities came there less to be seen than to see and hear entertainers who were more subtle and sophisticated than other clubs offered. The bar at the Gala was predominantly gay. The style that most homosexuals aspired to at that time was smart attire, refined tastes and discreet behavior.

One could hear Cole Porter tunes at the Gala before they were done on Broadway. Porter, who was one of the club's biggest boosters, gave his songs to Walsh so he could hear them performed by various artists. When he was in Hollywood the composer used to sit at the table which was reserved in his name with his own bottle of Cutty Sark in front of him. His date for the evening was usually Lady Sylvia Ashley-Fairbanks.

Mary Pickford and Buddy Rogers fêted Lillian Gish at the Café Gala. When Barbara Hutton and Cary Grant gave a party for Kay Francis there, Tyrone Power and Annabella were among the guests. Lana Turner and husband Stephen Crane used to come to the Gala to hold hands and listen to the then-

unknown Bobby Short. When nutritionist Gaylord Hauser could talk Greta Garbo into a night on the town the Café Gala was their favorite spot. On one evening the patrons included Marlene Dietrich, with her lover Jean Gabin, Adrian, with wife Janet Gaynor, and Lady Mendl, who was escorted by William Somerset Maugham.

Artur Rubinstein and Igor Stravinsky led the parade of European artists and intellectuals who flocked to the Gala. Gloria Vanderbilt made it a favorite of the young American smart set.

Strict wartime regulations demanded that

shutters and heavy curtains be used to black out all light after a certain hour. It was then, after most of the customers and help had left, that John Walsh played host at small impromptu parties for such stars as Judy Garland, Lena Horne and Frank Sinatra.

"We'd play records, dance and sing together until the wee hours," recalled Walsh in 1980. "Some of the best shows were given after we had closed for the night."

In June of 1948 the Café Gala closed forever.

John Walsh with Edie of the famed piano team Edie and Rack. One of the features of the Gala was twin baby-grand pianos. After the Gala closed in 1948, Edie and Rack, who were married, went on to New York's Blue Angel nightclub.

John Walsh (center) with Billie Holiday and her accompanist at the Café Gala.

The Castle of the Fairy Lady

Paul Adrian 1980

Los Angeles Herald-Examiner

A view of Mount Kalmia taken from over its huge iron gates at 1486 Sweetzer, which is now the entrance to the castle.

Hersee Moody Carson on the terrace of her mansion during the thirties.

When it was completed it stood alone on a hill which its owner, a multimillionaire, named Mount Kalmia. The building itself was called Castle Kalmia until its mistress, Hersee Moody Carson, began a tradition which continued until her death in the early forties. By then it was well known as the Castle of the Fairy Lady.

The petite gray-haired woman, whose husband built the castle and then died leaving her millions of dollars, was a devout Christian. On every holiday busloads of youngsters, some who were orphans and others who were crippled, were brought to the castle, where caterers and clowns provided food and entertainment for them. As many as four hundred underprivileged youngsters at a time reveled in the hospitality of the childless Mrs. Carson, whom they affectionately referred to as the Fairy Lady.

The dessert at those parties was always the same—an enormous angel-food cake, shaped and decorated as the Holy Bible.

Mrs. Carson sent this hand-tinted Christmas card to all of her friends in 1940.

Bison Archives

Raymond Chandler

Many who have never been to Los Angeles feel they know the city from Raymond Chandler's descriptions of its architecture and its residents. His rather jaundiced views of Los Angeles are throughout his works. The mystery writer in many cases used real buildings in his stories. Sometimes he changed their names. Sometimes he didn't.

Chandler began writing mysteries in the early thirties. His first were published in *Black Mask* magazine. At that time he was living in an apartment at 4616 Greenwood Place.

Later Chandler lived at 857 Iliff Street near Sunset Boulevard and Chautauqua in Pacific Palisades. About 1943 his address was 6520 Drexel near Fairfax. While working on *The High Window* and *The Lady in the Lake*, Chandler lived at 12216 Shetland Lane in Brentwood.

The Bryson Apartments was the setting of some of the action in The Lady in the Lake. *It is at 2701 Wilshire Boulevard.*

Paul Adrian 1979

Paul Adrian 1979

The apartment house where the gambler-blackmailer "Joe Brody" was murdered in The Big Sleep was actually the building at the corner of Palmerston Place and Kenmore near Franklin Avenue. Chandler's main character, private detective "Philip Marlowe," may have taken over the "Brody" apartment at a reduced rent because of the crime that had been committed there. The arched entrances to the garages Chandler referred to are part of the building next door.

Sandy Brown Wyeth 1980

The Santa Monica Pier was where "Marlowe" rented the water taxi in Farewell, My Lovely to take him to "Laird Brunett's" gambling ship, the Montecito.

The Montecito, which is an apartment house at 6650 Franklin Avenue in Hollywood, Chandler called the Chateau Bercy in The Little Sister. That book was filmed under the title Marlowe (1969) at the Hotel Alvarado at 6065 West 6th Street. Another building that figured prominently in The Little Sister was the Hotel Van Nuys. That hotel is now called the Barclay. The "V.N." can still be seen in its glass doors at 103 West 4th. It was at the Van Nuys that "George Hicks" received an ice pick in his neck.

Paul Adrian 1979

Charlie Chaplin

When Charlie Chaplin left Mack Sennett he built his own studio at 1416 North La Brea Avenue in Hollywood. The first picture he made there was *A Dog's Life* (1918). *The Gold Rush* (1925), *City Lights* (1931), *Modern Times* (1936) and *The Great Dictator* (1940) were also produced at that facility.

Since fans often collected around the entrance of the studio, Chaplin usually used the side door around the corner on DeLongpre near La Brea.

Chaplin purchased the land in 1918 for $35,000 and sold it in 1953 for $650,000.

For approximately ten years the lot was owned by American-International Pictures. Stanley Kramer, too, had his offices there. The studio is now the headquarters of A&M Records.

Most of Chaplin's Hollywood years were spent in the mansion he built at 1085 Summit Drive in Beverly Hills. Both of Charlie's sons were born there. The comedian lived in the high-ceilinged Georgian house with three wives: Lita Grey Chaplin, Paulette Goddard and Oona O'Neil.

The Home of Charles Chaplin, Beverly Hills, California.

This 1923 postcard shows the home Chaplin was living in at that time. It states incorrectly that it was in Beverly Hills. The house was in Hollywood at 6147 Temple Hill Drive and looks exactly the same today.

May McAvoy lived there after Chaplin. Then Mary Astor took it and lived there during her affair with John Barrymore.

When Chaplin's sons Sydney and Charles, Jr., returned from service after World War II they took over the Circle Theatre at 800 El Centro in Hollywood. It was they who turned it into a theater-in-the-round, one of the early examples of such staging in the United States. One of their partners in the venture was the son of Bob Burns, known on radio and in movies as the Arkansas Traveler.

The large house at the corner of Sunset Boulevard and La Brea where Sydney Chaplin lived was torn down and replaced by a supermarket in the mid-fifties. The tennis court that adjoined the house where the Chaplin brothers often played went at the same time.

Ciro's

The two big Hollywood nightclubs of the forties and fifties were Charlie Morrison's Mocombo, which was at 8588 Sunset Boulevard, and Ciro's, at 8433 Sunset Boulevard.

The "Mo," as it was often called, is long gone. Ciro's is now the Comedy Store.

During the heyday of Ciro's, Herman Hover presided over the glamour, the gushing and the gaucheries.

Ciro's played one top act only—headliners such as Mae West and her musclemen, Martin and Lewis, and Maurice Chevalier. Sometimes Hover made an exception, such as when Janis Paige had Sammy Davis, Jr., as her opening act. And there were always the "Ciro's Girls." Barbara Eden was one.

Ciro's was where dapper Franchot Tone spat in the face of gossip columnist Florabel Muir. It's where Johnny Weissmuller tipped a table filled with food onto Lupe Velez. When Darryl F. Zanuck gave a party for his daughter at Ciro's the production chief of 20th Century-Fox swung over the heads of four hundred guests on a trapeze. Sonja Henie was a regular. So was Howard Hughes.

Paul Adrian

FRANCHOT TONE JAILED AFTER ROW AT CIRO'S

Actor Spat in Her Face, Columnist Charges in Battery Complaint

And it was at Ciro's that Errol Flynn went to settle a score with Hollywood commentator Jimmy Fidler, who hid under the table to avoid him. Finally Mrs. Fidler stabbed Flynn in the ear with a fork. When that happened the band switched from a rhumba to "The Star-Spangled Banner." Everyone then stood up, including Fidler, who in so doing gave his head a terrible whack.

Hover followed the bleeding Errol Flynn into the men's room and told him in no uncertain terms what Ciro's policy was: "You've had one fight here before, Errol," said Hover. "There's a limit of three. Better pick your next one carefully."

Hover always insisted that gentlemen wear coats and ties. After all, it was Ciro's.

Nat King Cole

Nat King Cole bought the English Tudor mansion at 401 South Muirfield Road for $85,000 as a wedding present for his bride, Maria, in 1948. Mrs. Cole was duly surprised and pleased. Their new neighbors, however, were shocked and angry.

The twelve-room house is in an area of large, costly homes known as Larchmont. Although it is close to three of Hollywood's major studios, very few members of the entertainment industry have ever lived there.

Larchmont residents called a property owners' meeting shortly after the Coles moved in. An attorney for the group summed up its feelings when he said that many of those present were born and raised in Larchmont: "We are greatly disturbed at the prospect of having undesirables living here."

Cole responded: "I'm relieved to hear how concerned you all are about your neighborhood. I feel exactly the same way. I'd like you all to know that if my wife or I see anyone undesirable in Larchmont we'll be the first to object. Thank you."

After the death of Nat King Cole in 1965, Mrs. Cole sold the house to a family of wealthy blacks.

Nat "King" Cole had just raised his price to $50 a week when he and the other members of his trio began an engagement at the Swanee Inn. Up until that time they each were making $35 weekly. Nat was the pianist of the group.

One evening a regular customer asked for a particular tune and specified that it be sung. None of the three sang. The customer insisted. Finally Cole, explaining that he really didn't sing and didn't know the lyrics of the song requested, offered to do "Sweet Lorraine."

That was the beginning of the career of a vocalist who was to be called "in a class by himself." He recorded "Sweet Lorraine" in 1943. It was the fifth record he ever made.

The Swanee Inn has moved a few doors north of where it was in the forties. It is now located at 143 North La Brea. The original was where the inn's parking lot is now.

The night the world first heard Nat King Cole sing he received from that customer a fifteen-cent tip.

Paul Adrian 1979

Paul Adrian 1979

Russ Columbo

Singer Russ Columbo seemed on the brink of major stardom when he and Carole Lombard watched the preview of his latest picture on Friday evening, August 31, 1934. He had just signed with NBC for his own coast-to-coast radio program and with Warner Bros. to star in two movies. His recordings of "Prisoner of Love" and "Paradise" were the hits of the day. He was living at 1940 Outpost Circle, just off Hollywood Boulevard, and was rumored to be engaged to Carole, who had recently divorced William Powell.

But over that weekend Columbo and Carole had a quarrel. Russ went to talk it over with his best friend, photographer Lansing V. Brown. The two were sitting at opposite ends of the desk in Brown's adobe house at 916 North Genesee in West Hollywood. Brown was toying with an antique French dueling pistol. There was a burst of light and a fragment of a bullet loaded in the gun many years before hit the desk top. It ricocheted into Columbo's left eye, passing to the brain, where it lodged. Within a few hours he was dead at age twenty-six. The date was Sunday, September 2, 1934.

Paul Adrian 1979

Just two days before he was killed, Russ Columbo's mother had suffered a heart attack. Afraid that the shock of the news might kill her, the Columbo family wrote her weekly letters with simulated European postmarks. Mrs. Columbo believed Russ was on a world tour. Once a month a check was enclosed. The money was taken from his insurance benefits.

Mrs. Columbo survived her son by nearly ten years. Her last words were, "Tell Russ how happy and proud he has made me."

Paul Adrian 1979

Dorothy Comingore

Dorothy Comingore gave a memorable performance as "Susan Alexander," the talentless singer in Orson Welles' *Citizen Kane* (1941). In the movie she ends up an alcoholic performing in a sleazy Atlantic City nightclub.

In March of 1953, the Los Angeles Sheriff's Vice Squad arrested Dorothy Comingore for prostitution after, they claimed, she had offered herself to them for "a lousy $10" in a bar at 8279 Santa Monica Boulevard in West Hollywood.

The actress vehemently denied the charge, which was later dismissed when she was committed to a clinic for treatment of alcoholism.

The bar was once called the Try Later and was owned by Frankie Darro, the star of B pictures. It is now the Raincheck.

It was one of Veronica Lake's favorite hangouts.

Joan Crawford

Joan Crawford first came to Hollywood on the Sunset Limited, leaving Kansas City on New Year's Day, 1925. Signed to a $75-a-week M-G-M contract, she first lived at the Hotel Washington at 3927 Van Buren in Culver City. It is within walking distance of the studio. Joan lived there until Metro picked up her first option and raised her salary to $100 a week.

In Bob Thomas' book *Joan Crawford,* he wrote about her visits as a young M-G-M contract player in 1925 to St. Augustine's Roman Catholic Church at 3850 Jasmine in Culver City: "Each morning before she reported to the studio, Joan stopped at the tiny church across Washington Boulevard. She prayed that her hard work at the studio would be rewarded with stardom and that she would someday find the love that had eluded her from her earliest years."

Steven Arnold 1980

Steven Arnold 1980

Joan bought the property at 426 North Bristol in Brentwood for $40,000 in 1929. Behind the high wall and gates is a large white stucco Moorish house. She lived there with her first three husbands: Douglas Fairbanks, Jr., Franchot Tone and Phillip Terry. It is in this home that most of what was described by her adopted daughter, Christina, in *Mommie Dearest* took place.

Later in her life Joan Crawford rented an apartment at 8313 Fountain Avenue in West Hollywood. The building was owned by Loretta Young, who also lived there.

JAN·24·46

MAY THIS CEMENT OUR FRIENDSHIP.

Joan Crawford

9-14-29

Joan Crawford was one of the first stars to have her prints and signature in the forecourt of Grauman's Chinese Theatre.

Joan Crawford's star is just north of Hollywood Boulevard in front of the entrance of Capitol Records at 1750 Vine Street in Hollywood.

Joan Crawford purchased this Cadillac V-16 Town Car new for $7,500 in 1933. It was one of the three such models built that year.

The automobile, which has been completely restored, is owned by Hillcrest Motor Company of Beverly Hills, the original dealer. It is on public display.

In 1962 Joan Crawford and Bette Davis were co-starred in Whatever Happened to Baby Jane?, *which was filmed mainly at 172 North McCadden Place in Los Angeles. The house looks almost the same today, including the iron gates across the driveway. It was there that the early talkie star "Blanche Hudson" (Joan Crawford) was run over by a car driven by her younger sister "Jane" (Bette Davis).*

Marion Davies

Sandy Brown Wyeth 1980

The Los Altos at 4121 Wilshire Boulevard was one of the first cooperative apartment houses on the West Coast. Marion Davies led the parade of motion picture personalities who lived there. Her six-bathroom suite had a marbled entrance and a screening room.

Marion Davies was one of the wealthiest and most colorful stars in the history of Hollywood. Yet those who knew her well liked her for her warmth and sincerity. There are no unpleasant Marion Davies stories in Hollywood. Tennessee Williams said about her after their first meeting, "She makes up for the rest of Hollywood."

When Marion Davies first came to Hollywood she lived for a while at the Hollywood Hotel.

Her mansion at 1700 Lexington Road in Beverly Hills was where King Vidor and Eleanor Boardman were married in what was planned as a double ceremony in 1926. John Gilbert and Greta Garbo were to be wed at the same time, but Garbo never showed up. After Marion sold it the house was lived in by movie mogul Harry Cohn.

Marion later lived at 1011 Beverly Drive, a house which cannot be seen from the road. John F. Kennedy spent his honeymoon at this estate, and his father, Joseph P. Kennedy, took it over during the 1960 Democratic Convention. It was here that the elder Kennedy watched his son on television accepting the nomination for the Presidency.

No visit by a dignitary to Metro-Goldwyn-Mayer was complete without a lunch at Marion Davies' "bungalow," shown here in the late twenties. General MacArthur, Winston Churchill, former President Calvin Coolidge and George Bernard Shaw were a few of those she fêted. When Marion left M-G-M for Warner Bros., a distance of over twenty miles, the two-story structure followed her.

Many of the stars had luxurious houses along the "Gold Coast," land which is between the Pacific Coast Highway and the Pacific Ocean in Santa Monica. But Ocean House, the Marion Davies compound, was the largest and most lavish of all.

The main house had fifty-five bathrooms, thirty-seven fireplaces and a 110-foot swimming pool which was lined with Italian marble.

Construction of the Georgian-style mansion was begun in 1926 and completed in 1930, at a cost of $3 million. The balustrades alone took the efforts of seventy-five craftsmen carving for a full year. Some of the ceilings were excellent reproductions of old drawings. One was an eighteenth-century fresco imported from a London town house. The furnishings cost $4 million.

The dining room, reception room and drawing room, each of which was sixty feet in length, were brought from Burton Hall,

The Marion Davies compound in Santa Monica just before and just after the main buildings were razed in 1956.

An aerial view of Ocean House taken in the mid-thirties.

County Clare, Ireland. The projection room featured a screen that rose from the floor and a seventeenth-century mantel of carved oak.

There was a "rathskeller" on the lower level, where the more intimate parties were held. It had originally been not a rathskeller but an inn in Surrey, England, that dated back to 1560.

In Marion's suite on the second floor there was a marble mantel adorned with wine-drinking cherubs which had once been in a mansion built in England in 1760.

Thirty-two servants looked after their mistress and the world figures who were her guests.

In 1947 Marion Davies sold the property for $600,000.

In 1956 the main house was demolished. All that remains now of what was once known as the Versailles of Hollywood is a private beach club at 415 Palisades Beach Road.

ul Adrian 1979

Sandy Brown Wyeth 1979

The columns in front of the building at 9370 Santa Monica Boulevard in Beverly Hills were originally part of Marion Davies' Ocean House.

Marion Davies was born on January 3, 1897, and died in 1961. She was laid to rest in a solid bronze casket covered with pink carnations and orchids. Her mausoleum, which bears her original family name of Douras, is across from the Cathedral Mausoleum at Hollywood Memorial Park Cemetery.

Hannah Chaplin, the mother of Charlie Chaplin, is buried to the left of the Marion Davies tomb. Tyrone Power's grave is to the right.

James Dean

James Dean was a UCLA student living in the Sigma Nu House at 601 Gayley in Westwood until he was expelled for punching a fraternity brother during a beer party.

Dean then lived for a while at the Gower Plaza Hotel at 1607 North Gower in Hollywood. At the time he worked nearby at CBS Radio, 6121 Sunset Boulevard.

Dean shared an apartment with Richard Davalos when the two were playing brothers in *East of Eden* (1955). The apartment building was at 3908 Barham Boulevard, directly across the street from Warner Bros. Studio, where the film was made.

Paul Adrian 1979

Paul Adrian 1979

Paul Adrian 1979

Paul Adrian 1979

Albert Dekker

Albert Dekker was known as a distinguished character actor on the Broadway stage and in over two hundred movies. On the screen he was most effective as a villain. Some of his best-known pictures were *Man in the Iron Mask* (1939), *Seven Sinners* (1940), *The Killers* (1946) and *East of Eden* (1955).

Dekker had a keen interest in politics and served as the Democratic state assemblyman from California's 57th District from 1944 to 1946.

Albert Dekker's other life was a well-kept secret, unknown even to his children and the woman to whom he was engaged at the time of his death.

The sixty-two-year-old actor was found by Los Angeles police on May 5, 1968, when they broke into his locked bathroom at 1731 North Normandie. He was hanging by a rope harness which had been tied around his neck and then over the shower pipe. A single handcuff was locked on both of his wrists and he was tightly bound all over in ropes. Hypodermic marks were on his body in a number of places, and two hypodermic needles were still in him. He wore no clothing but was covered in obscenities which were written on his skin in his own hand. The Los Angeles coroner listed the death as "accidental," since there was no evidence he had intended to commit suicide.

The police called it "quite an unusual case."

Paul Adrian 1979

Marlene Dietrich

Charlie Mack of the team Murray and Mack lived at 822 North Roxbury Drive in Beverly Hills while the pair were riding the crest of their popularity in vaudeville and on radio as *The Two Black Crows*.

Marlene Dietrich took the house over from Mack after the Lindbergh baby was kidnapped in 1932. That crime triggered a wave of threatened and attempted kidnappings in Hollywood. Dietrich was sufficiently disturbed by an unsigned note she received to move with her daughter, Maria, to this house at the corner of Roxbury Drive and Sunset Boulevard. The bars she had put on all the windows are still there.

Fans knew Marlene was at home when her blue Rolls-Royce roadster was parked in the driveway.

Paul Adrian 1979

Paul Adrian 1979

Walt Disney

Paul Adrian 1980

When Walt Disney first came to town in 1923 he roomed with his uncle at 4406 Kingswell near Vermont. It was in the garage at the rear of that property that Disney did his first work in Hollywood.

On October 16, 1923, Disney signed to produce a series of shorts and rented space in the back room of the business at 4651 Kingswell for $10 a month. In February 1924, his company, which was at that time known as Disney Brothers Studio, moved next door to 4649 Kingswell.

In July 1925, the Disneys put down a deposit on a lot at 2719 Hyperion Avenue. By mid-February 1926, they had moved into their new facilities. It remained the home of Walt Disney Studios until May 1940, when the company occupied its present site at 500 South Buena Vista in Burbank. The Hyperion studio site is now a shopping center.

The garage at 4406 Kingswell where Walt Disney did his first work in Hollywood in 1923.

© Walt Disney Productions

The studio Disney built at 2719 Hyperion in 1925–26 is no longer standing. This is where Mickey Mouse was created in 1928, followed within a few years by Pluto, Goofy and Donald Duck. Snow White and the Seven Dwarfs was produced here.

The Hotel Dunbar is now a historical monument housing a black museum on its main floor. The vacant lot to the right is where the Club Alabam once stood.

In 1974, three decades after its heyday ended, the Hotel Dunbar at 4225 South Central Avenue was declared an historical monument. Built in 1928, it was named for Paul Laurence Dunbar, a well-known black poet who died in 1906.

The Dunbar was the place to see black celebrities. The Clark Hotel, a few blocks away at Central Avenue and Washington Boulevard, was somewhat more staid. It drew black society, but when Bill "Bojangles" Robinson or Joe Louis was in town they stopped at the Dunbar. Any black who was anyone in entertainment or sports came to the Dunbar.

Although whites did not stay at the Dunbar, any more than blacks stayed in white hotels then, they were there to cast shows and movies. They came also to see the shows at the Club Alabam.

The Club Alabam was next door to the hotel and headlined some of the biggest black acts of the time. Count Basie, Dinah Washington, Duke Ellington and, early in his career, Nat King Cole are only a few of the stars who played the Alabam. That building was torn down years ago.

Deanna Durbin

Easter Love Song

VAUGHN PAUL.   DEANNA DURBIN.
Smilingly apply for license to marry.

DEANNA DURBIN FILES TO MARRY

Songbird and Her Girlhood Beau Apply

Easter Bonnets Won't Get Wet

Weatherman Says Storm to Hold Off

Universal Pictures was on the verge of bankruptcy when their teenage contractee Deanna Durbin became a box-office sensation. It happened almost overnight in the picture *Three Smart Girls* (1937).

When she married her first husband, studio executive Vaughn Paul, front pages across the nation featured the couple. The newlyweds settled into the big white house at 7922 Hollywood Boulevard near Laurel Canyon.

Paul Adrian 1979

Peg Entwistle

Paul Adrian 1979

The world-famous Hollywood sign originally read "Hollywoodland." It was erected on the side of Mount Lee by promoters of an unsuccessful real estate venture in 1923.

Starlet Peg Entwistle was fascinated by that sign, according to her uncle, with whom she lived at 2428 Beachwood Drive. She rode horseback daily in the hills beneath it.

Peg Entwistle came to Hollywood with high hopes for breaking into the movies. After leaving her native England she appeared in several Broadway plays. One of those who admired her work on the stage was ingenue Bette Davis. In Hollywood Peg signed a contract with RKO Pictures and was seen in several RKO films. But in July of 1932 the studio decided not to pick up her option.

After that Peg would stand at the gate of her uncle's home gazing up Beachwood Drive at the sign.

On the evening of Friday, September 16, 1932, Peg Entwistle told her uncle she was going out for some cigarettes. She never returned. Wearing a dress she had borrowed from Broadway leading lady Effie Shannon, Peg climbed up the side of the mountain and onto the fifty-foot-high H. From there she jumped to her death.

Steven Arnold 1980

Paul Adrian 1979

Ruth Etting

Ruth Etting, singing star of the *Ziegfeld Follies,* radio and the movies, had her story made into a technicolor musical called *Love Me or Leave Me* (1955). Doris Day played Ruth and James Cagney was her husband-manager, Moe "the Gimp" Snyder. Myrl Alderman, her arranger-accompanist, was portrayed by Cameron Mitchell.

Contrary to the movie, Snyder did not leap from the bushes in front of Alderman's home and shoot him. On that fateful night of October 15, 1938, Ruth Etting, who had recently divorced Snyder and moved in with Alderman, was preparing a dinner of pork chops and vegetables. She looked out of the window at the far right and saw Snyder and Alderman emerge from the latter's car. Once inside the house Snyder demanded to know if Ruth and Alderman were lovers. When she told him that was none of his business Snyder shot Alderman.

The house where it all happened is off Barham Boulevard at 3090 Lake Hollywood Drive in the Hollywood Knolls section of Los Angeles.

Paul Adrian 1979

W. C. Fields

W. C. Fields always rented the homes he lived in. In 1932 he took a lease on the five-acre ranch at White Oak Avenue in Encino. The estate, which was for a while owned by Don Ameche, had pomegranate trees, an orange grove and an aviary. His friends William Le Baron, head of Paramount Pictures, Gregory La Cava, the director, and writer Gene Fowler were usually at the small parties Fields gave on Sundays.

An excellent tennis player, Fields took delight in beating his cronies on the court beside his house. This property has since been subdivided.

In 1936 Fields and his companion Carlotta Monti moved from Encino to 655 Funchall Road in Bel Air. The three-acre estate was offered to him at the time for $25,000, but the comedian did not want the responsibility of owning property.

It was in this house that impresario Earl Carroll gave Fields a surprise birthday party.

Director Eddie Sutherland, Dorothy Lamour and Edgar Bergen were frequent guests.

Fields' good friend John Barrymore lived nearby in this secluded house at 11000 Bellagio Road. Barrymore and his wife, Elaine Barrie, called their home La Vida Nueva (The New Life). "The Great Profile" often would walk up the hill in the evening for long talks with W. C. Fields.

The Garden of Allah

Nazimova, one of Hollywood's first superstars, was being paid $13,000 a week to act in silent films when she moved into the mansion at 8152 Sunset Boulevard. It was surrounded by three and a half acres of poplar, cedar and fruit trees.

During her brief reign no one in filmdom had more influence on the life-style of motion picture stars than Nazimova. Her guests called her "Madame" and were forbidden to ever bid her "good night," a phrase she believed brought bad luck. She had a "moon parlor," a swimming pool shaped like the Black Sea and a protégée named Natacha Rambova who became the wife of Rudolph Valentino. She was also the godmother of Nancy Reagan.

Nazimova presided over Hollywood's social scene along with her director-lover, Charles Bryant, until she began to slip badly at the box office during the early twenties. Although she sold her interest in the property, the new owners allowed her to maintain a small apartment on the second floor rent-free as long as she lived. She saw her gardens of semitropical flowers replaced by twenty-five guest cottages as her former home became a hotel. The cruelest blow of all was its name, the Garden of Allah. Nazimova's first name was spelled "Alla."

The swimming pool of the Garden of Allah in 1946.

Bison Archives

Orson Welles lived at the Garden of Allah when he was working on *Journey into Fear* (1942). It was there he had an affair with Lili St. Cyr. His apartment was directly beneath Nazimova's. When his dictation or his secretary's typing went on too late at night "Madame" would thump on the floor with her cane.

By the time she died in 1945 at the age of sixty-six the hotel had become a haven for hard-drinking celebrities such as Errol Flynn, Dorothy Parker, Robert Benchley and F. Scott Fitzgerald.

The hotel and cottages, which were demolished in 1959 to make way for a savings and loan company, were reproduced in miniature and are displayed under glass on the original site near the corner of Crescent Heights Boulevard and Sunset Boulevard.

The facade of the Garden of Allah in 1947.

The former site of the Garden of Allah now displays miniatures of the hotel and its cottages under glass.

Ava Gardner

Ava Gardner first came to Hollywood in 1941. She was eighteen years old and had just been placed under contract to Metro-Goldwyn-Mayer at a salary of $75 a week. Her first address was the Hollywood Wilcox Hotel across from the post office.

The Hotel Hollywood Wilcox at Selma and Wilcox.

Paul Adrian 1979

Judy Garland

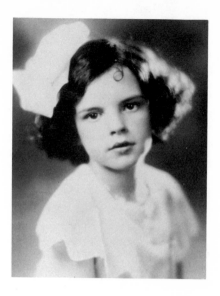

Judy Garland's name was Frances Gumm when she first arrived in Hollywood in 1926. The Gumm family stayed for about two weeks at the St. Moritz Hotel at 5849 Sunset Boulevard. At that time the Warner Bros. studio was directly across the street.

Once the Gumms settled in Hollywood Judy was enrolled at the Lawlor School at 5400 Hollywood Boulevard. When she was a student that school for performing children occupied the second floor of the building which later became the Hollywood Professional School. Among Judy's classmates then were Mickey Rooney, Frankie Darro and Baby Peggy Montgomery.

After Judy was placed under contract to Metro-Goldwyn-Mayer on October 15, 1935, she was tutored in the studio's "Little Red Schoolhouse." In this photo Elizabeth Taylor and Dean Stockwell are among the movie moppets standing outside with their teacher. The building is now used as offices and has been renamed the Crawford Building.

Judy Garland's first Los Angeles home was at 3154 Glen Manor Place in the Atwater district.

She next lived at 2605 Ivanhoe Drive in the Silverlake area.

Paul Adrian 1979   Paul Adrian 1979

In 1934 the Gumms, who had rented until then, bought the house at 2671 Lakeview Terrace East.

Judy's fourth home was a cottage in the rear of 1222½ North Normandie in Los Angeles.

Then her family resided on the second floor of a flat at 1814½ South Orchard near Washington Boulevard.

842 North Mariposa, where they next lived, has been replaced by an apartment house.

Just after Judy Garland was signed to her first M-G-M contract in 1935 the family moved into 180 South McCadden Place near Beverly Boulevard.

It was in the house at 10000 Sunset Boulevard that Judy Garland recuperated from a suicide attempt. Judy was separated at the time from her second husband, director Vincente Minnelli.

William Haines

The handsome edifice at 8720 Sunset Boulevard on "the Strip" was built in 1934 for William Haines, the perennial smart aleck of the silent screen. After Haines' career began to wane in the early thirties he and his lover Jimmy Shields went into the interior decorating business with the blessings and commissions of his close friend and former co-star Joan Crawford.

Montgomery Management Co.

In June of 1936, Haines and Shields were dragged through a barrage of the worst sort of publicity when the parents of a six-year-old boy accused a man who was a guest at the Haines beach house of molesting their son. Haines' home at 221 Moonstone Street in El Porto was marched on by some one hundred townspeople who called themselves the "White Legion." Haines, Shields and their houseguests were literally driven out of the town after being pelted with garbage and beaten.

Although he suffered emotionally, Haines' business prospered. Joan Crawford continued to rely on his taste, as did many other Hollywood personalities and establishments such as the Mocombo. Until he died in 1973 the Haines touch was sought by the rich and powerful.

Perhaps the crowning achievement of his second career was decorating and refurbishing the United States Embassy in London.

The former William Haines studio is now Le Dome, one of Hollywood's most fashionable restaurants.

Paul Adrian 1979

Hollywood Canteen

Nowhere in Hollywood—perhaps nowhere in the United States—was civilian support of servicemen during World War II more enthusiastic than at the Hollywood Canteen. Movie stars not only entertained the boys and danced with them, they served them meals and then washed the dishes. Men and women in uniforms of all the armed services came to hear Judy Garland sing while Jose Iturbi played, or to chat with Deanna Durbin, or to ask Joan Crawford to help them write letters to the folks back home.

The Canteen brought together stars who might never have met. Dinah Shore and George Montgomery had been introduced before they ran into each other at the Canteen, but it was there that they "clicked."

Bette Davis and John Garfield conceived the idea of the Hollywood Canteen, which all of the motion picture industry supported wholeheartedly.

The converted barn where it all took place was torn down in 1966 and a five-story garage now stands in its place at 1451 North Cahuenga Boulevard, just south of Sunset Boulevard.

Paul Adrian 1979

Irene Manning was making The Desert Song *with Dennis Morgan when she spent Christmas Eve, 1943, passing out presents to the boys at the Hollywood Canteen.*

Slapsie Maxie Rosenbloom beside the list of performers who were killed or injured while entertaining U.S. troops during World War II.

HONOR ROLL

+ CAROLE LOMBARD
+ LESLIE HOWARD
+ ROY ROGNAN
+ TAMARA
+ CHARLES KING
+ BOB RIPA

INJURED

JANE FROMAN
GYPSY MARKOFF
GRACE DRYSDALE

Just a small sample of the stars who entertained our GIs at the Hollywood Canteen are (left to right) Danny Kaye, Charles Boyer, Betty Grable, Harry James, John Garfield, Bette Davis, Jimmy Durante, Ronald Colman, Roddy McDowall, Sophie Tucker, Anne Dvorak, Hedy Lamarr, Mickey Rooney, Jennifer Jones.

More of the stars who made the Hollywood Canteen a favorite stop for U.S. men and women in service are (left to right) Frank Morgan, Deanna Durbin, Nelson Eddy, Ginger Rogers, Frank Sinatra, Kay Kyser, Martha Raye, Walter Pidgeon, Dinah Shore, Rudy Vallee, Jack Carson, Jose Iturbi, Judy Garland.

Hollywood Hotel

The Hollywood Hotel in 1949.

The Hollywood Hotel was the first and only "grand hotel" Hollywood ever had. It was already well established before the city became the world's movie capital.

During the early twenties the world's most famous stars and directors dined and danced at the Hollywood Hotel. On Thursday evening was their weekly dinner dance. Lionel Barrymore could be seen dancing with Pauline Frederick, although Francis X. Bushman might cut in. Mary Pickford tried to make Thursdays her "night out" unless she had an early call the next morning.

Rudolph Valentino not only was a habitué, he married his first wife, Jean Acker, at the hotel in 1919, and that is where they spent their honeymoon.

Fatty Arbuckle lived there for a while, as did Elinor Glyn, the best-selling novelist of the day and the woman who made the word "It" synonymous with sex appeal. Madame Glyn, as everyone called her, held court on the hotel's large veranda. Seated in a peacock chair, she would dispense good advice to her avid followers such as Aileen Pringle and Gloria Swanson.

The Hollywood Hotel was on the northwest corner of Hollywood Boulevard and Highland Avenue. It was razed in 1956 to make way for the office building that is there today.

The Hollywood Hotel was razed in 1956.

The former sight of the Hollywood Hotel, Hollywood Boulevard at Highland Avenue.

The House of Francis

Like the good newspaperman he was, H. L. Mencken sought out the city's real powers when he made his well-publicized visit to the film capital in 1926. Lee Francis, already established as Hollywood's classiest madam, was one of the first personalities he asked to meet. The Baltimore oracle drove over to Lee's in a Rolls-Royce he borrowed from Tom Mix and played a few pieces on her piano. He found her a "fine lady" and swore he ventured no farther than her parlor.

Mencken was probably the only man who ever remained downstairs in any of Lee's "places." And he was certainly the only one who talked about his visit for publication. The married men and movie stars, world-famous for their sexual attractiveness, hardly wanted it known that they were paying money to spend time with prostitutes. It was not what the public expected of their male idols such as Errol Flynn, a loyal client of the House of Francis.

Because of the nature of Lee Francis' profession she moved frequently, usually operating within the area of the Strip. But the law did once catch up with her when she was raided on January 16, 1940.

"You're a sly one, you are," said Lee as the arresting officer led her away. "In thirty-one years in the business this is the first time anyone ever got me."

She was found guilty of keeping a house of ill repute in a large apartment at 8439 Sunset Boulevard, next door to Ciro's. Her sentence of thirty days was slightly reduced by the warden, who found her "a model inmate." Lee spent the time behind bars writing her life story, *Ladies on Call.*

The building where Lee Francis was finally brought to justice is now owned by rock star Rod Stewart.

Howard Hughes

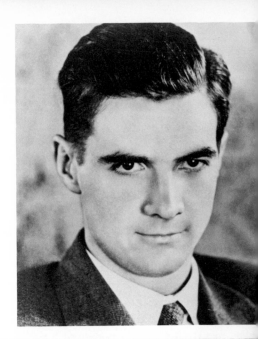

Howard Hughes' first Hollywood home was at 211 Muirfield Road. Old-timers in the neighborhood still remember watching Hughes on Sunday afternoons practicing his golf strokes on the front lawn with a luscious blonde. The girl was Jean Harlow, whom he made a star in *Hell's Angels* (1930).

His last Hollywood home was behind the iron gates at 1001 Bel Air Road in Bel Air. He lived there with his wife at the time, Jean Peters.

Paul Adrian 1979

Paul Adrian 1979

The Hughes offices were always in the Art Deco building at 7000 Romaine Avenue in Hollywood. It is there his films such as *Scarface* (1932) and *The Outlaw* (1949) were edited.

Paul Adrian 1979

The main entrance to RKO Studios in 1949. Some of the stars who used to pass through these doors almost daily were Fred Astaire, Ginger Rogers, Irene Dunne, Jane Russell and Helen Twelvetrees. When she first came to the studio Katharine Hepburn used to sit on the steps and read her fan mail.

Howard Hughes owned controlling interest in RKO Studios as well as RKO Theatres from May 11, 1948, until he sold out on July 18, 1955. This photo shows the main entrance to the studio at 780 North Gower in Hollywood when it was a major lot. It was run at various times by Joseph P. Kennedy (the father of the late President), David O. Selznick and Dore Schary. For a while it was owned by Desi Arnaz and Lucille Ball and was called Desilu.

The entire RKO lot is now owned and occupied by Paramount Pictures. What was the RKO main entrance is now Paramount's side door.

Los Angeles Times

ALL THE NEWS
ALL THE TIME

9 A.M. FINAL

DAILY, FIVE CENTS.

HOWARD HUGHES CRITICAL
Millionaire Flyer Given 50-50 Chance
Plane Hits 4 Houses in Beverly Hills

On July 7, 1946, Dennis O'Keefe was looking out the window of his Beverly Hills home at 802 North Linden Drive and saw an experimental Army photographic plane go out of control and plunge downward. It tore off more than half the roof from 803 North Linden Drive, and its right wing sliced through the upstairs bedroom of number 805.

Rosemary De Camp, who lived directly behind those homes, received a minor burn on one of her hands. The other residents of the four houses involved were miraculously untouched.

The plane's pilot, Howard Hughes, hovered near death for days after he was pulled out of the flaming wreckage. Hughes never fully recovered from the injuries he sustained in that crash. It was the beginning of the drug usage that was to plague him for the rest of his life.

Paul Adrian 1979

Paul Adrian 1979

Al Jolson

When Al Jolson and Ruby Keeler returned from their honeymoon in 1928, Al carried Ruby over the threshold into their new home at 4875 Louise in Encino. The recent bride is reclining on the lawn in this photograph.

After a long career, Al Jolson died of a heart attack in 1950 at the age of sixty-four while playing gin rummy in his suite at the St. Francis Hotel in San Francisco.

Twenty thousand fans converged on Temple Israel in Los Angeles to hear George Jessel, the man who turned down the starring role in *The Jazz Singer*, deliver Jolson's eulogy.

Later Jessel said of his rival, "He was a no-good son of a bitch but he was also the greatest entertainer I've ever seen."

It took three years to build Al Jolson's tomb at the Hillside Memorial Cemetery at 6001 Centinella near the Los Angeles International Airport. Floodlights illuminate the shrine, which can be seen night and day from the San Diego Freeway.

Beside the bronze sarcophagus is a nearly life-size statue of Jolson on one knee with arms outstretched.

Jolson's friends Jack Benny and Eddie Cantor are entombed in the building behind his resting place.

Paul Adrian 1980

69

Buck Jones

Duesenberg with gold-plated dashboard and door handles.

Tom Mix had paid little attention to Buck Jones when the latter was his double. Once Buck became a star, Mix turned outright hostile. But after a time the two western stars became close friends and Mix was a familiar face around Hacienda del Charro. They had a drink together at the big western bar in the Jones house on October 11, 1940. The next day Mix was killed in an auto crash.

One struggling actor who came by the estate often was a young man everyone called Tiny until he married his agent, Sue Carol. She insisted everyone call him Alan— Alan Ladd.

Bill "Hopalong Cassidy" Boyd was an old friend of Jones, as was Wallace Beery, whose nephew, Noah Beery, Jr., married Jones' daughter Maxine at the house in 1940.

In the fall of 1942, Jones left his home for a personal-appearance tour. He was being honored by a group of theater owners at a party in Boston's Coconut Grove when a fire broke out. Buck, who was always the hero of his starring vehicles, went into the fire three times, saving several lives, before he collapsed. The blaze killed 491 people, and Buck Jones died as a result of the burns he received.

By the time the Buck Jones estate was ready for occupancy in 1937 the movie cowboy had spent $110,000 to build the house, garages, corral and stables. Silver as well as his other horses were kept on the property, which was originally a ten-acre peach orchard in Van Nuys, California.

To make the structure earthquake-proof Jones had heavy steel wire run between the bricks and steel beams set in the concrete foundation. Massive Spanish furniture rested on floors made of burled oak which had been imported from Japan.

His automobile, which could usually be seen parked in the driveway, was a $21,000

Noah Beery, Jr. (left), and his new bride, Buck Jones' daughter Maxine, were married at the Jones estate in 1940. The groom's uncle, Wallace Beery, is on the right.

Paul Adrian 1980

The letters B and J were forged in the gates on the Buck Jones estate, Hacienda del Charro, at 14050 Magnolia Boulevard at the corner of Hazeltine in Van Nuys. This photo was taken in early 1980 just before the house was torn down.

Paul Adrian 1980

The Buck Jones estate shortly after it was completed in 1937.

Percy Kilbride

Percy Kilbride was best known for his portrayal of "Pa Kettle," the bumpkin character in a motheaten sweater who used a rope to hold up his pants. The actor played the role opposite Marjorie Main in ten highly successful feature films, beginning with *The Egg and I* (1947).

Fans often didn't recognize Kilbride during his daily strolls around Hollywood because offscreen he was quite meticulous about his appearance.

Percy lived at 6650 Franklin in Hollywood. He was crossing the intersection of Yucca and Cherokee near his apartment one evening when he was hit by an automobile. The friend he was with, another actor, was killed instantly. Percy Kilbride died eight days later on December 11, 1964, at the age of seventy-six.

Barbara La Marr

BARBARA LA MARR
WITH GOD IN THE JOY AND BEAUTY OF YOUTH
1896   1926

Barbara La Marr was only fourteen years old when a judge ordered her to leave Los Angeles, giving as his reason that she was "too young and too beautiful to be adrift in the big city."

Barbara became known as "The Girl Who Was Too Beautiful." Her other steppingstone to stardom in silent pictures was the role of Douglas Fairbanks, Sr.'s, leading lady in *The Three Musketeers* (1921).

Barbara La Marr was considered to be a "fast liver." She was married five times and died when she was thirty years old. She left behind a home at 6672½ Whitley Terrace, a beach house in Malibu that was blown to smithereens in the picture *Inside Daisy Clover,* and an adopted son whom Zazu Pitts raised.

"The Girl Who Was Too Beautiful" is buried in the Cathedral Mausoleum of the Hollywood Memorial Park Cemetery around the corner from her friend and former neighbor Rudolph Valentino.

Laurel & Hardy

In 1934 Stan Laurel lived at 718 North Bedford Drive in Beverly Hills.

Paul Adrian 1979

Oliver Hardy was living at 621 Alta Drive in Beverly Hills during the early thirties.

Paul Adrian 1980

Stan Laurel built a seven-foot brick wall around his estate, Fort Laurel, in an effort to keep out process servers, newspaper reporters and the curious.

The gates are now gone and Fort Laurel has been turned into a private grammar school. Children study and play in Laurel's former home and yard.

The wishing well is across from the small fish pond where Stan Laurel used to study his scripts on hot days.

The address is 20213 Strathern in Canoga Park.

Laurel and Hardy were parked in front of one house throughout *A Perfect Day* (1929). That's the movie where try as they might the pair and their guests never leave for their picnic.

Fifty years later the house at 3120 Vera in Culver City was almost unchanged.

In *Big Business* (1929) Laurel and Hardy try in vain to sell James Finlayson a Christmas

tree—in the middle of summer. After Finlayson cuts their sample tree to pieces they proceed to tear his house apart.

That house is at 10281 Dunleer Drive in Los Angeles.

The Music Box (1932) won its producer, Hal Roach, an Academy Award for that year's Best Comedy Short Subject.

The famous stairs used by Laurel and Hardy in that classic movie are located at 929 Vendome Boulevard in the Silverlake area of Los Angeles.

The Hardy estate in Van Nuys was sold after "Babe's" death to bandleader Horace Heidt. Heidt demolished all the buildings on the property except the Hardy home

and replaced them with a large apartment complex. The house still stands at 14227 Magnolia Boulevard.

This photograph was taken in 1961 just before the "Fun Factory" was torn down. That was where Laurel and Hardy worked out many of their routines. It could seat 150 people and had projection equipment and a stage.

Standing from left to right: Horace Heidt, Lucille Hardy-Price, Eddie Baker, Madge Kennedy, Joyce Compton, Francis X. Bushman, Mrs. Bushman, Vivian Duncan, Beatrice Kay, Babe London and Chester Conklin. Jane Darwell is seated.

Oliver Hardy died in 1957 at the home of his mother-in-law at 5421 Auckland Avenue in North Hollywood.

Stan Laurel spent the last years of his life at the Oceana Hotel at 849 Ocean Avenue in Santa Monica, where he died in 1965.

The remains of Oliver Norvell Hardy are in Valhalla Memorial Park Cemetery, 10621 Victory Boulevard, in North Hollywood.

Like his partner, Stan Laurel was cremated. His ashes are at Forest Lawn Memorial Park in the Hollywood Hills.

Paul Adrian 1979

Paul Adrian 1979

Paul Adrian 1979

Liberace

Paul Adrian 1979

Liberace's piano-shaped swimming pool was for a while as famous as his mother and brother George.

At Christmastime his home in Sherman Oaks became the San Fernando Valley's equivalent of the Rockefeller Center Christmas tree.

Liberace moved from 1545 Valley Vista over twenty years ago because so many tourists rang his doorbell.

"I'm so glad you like the house," he'd say to them. "Because, after all—*you* bought it!"

Bela Lugosi

Bison Archives

Paul Adrian 1979

In 1934 Bela Lugosi was living in the rooming house which can be seen from the northwest corner of Hudson and Hollywood Boulevard.

From 1942 to 1952 the Lugosi family lived in the home he built on Whipple Street near Lankersheim Boulevard in North Hollywood. The building, which has since been torn down, was styled very much like a typical home in his native Hungary.

Another of the Lugosi houses is at 2227 Outpost Drive in Hollywood.

On August 16, 1956, the star died in his apartment at 5620 Harold Way in Hollywood.

As he requested, Bela Lugosi was buried in the high-collared cape he wore in his many portrayals of "Count Dracula." His resting place is at Holy Cross Cemetery, only a few yards from the grave of Bing Crosby.

Paul Adrian 1979

Paul Adrian 1979

Hattie McDaniel

Hattie McDaniel won the Best Supporting Actress Oscar for her performance in *Gone with the Wind* (1939). She was the first black actress to win that award.

She was known all over the world for her portrayal of maids and cooks; however, in real life Hattie employed a chauffeur, secretary and housekeeper. The interior of her large home at 2203 Harvard Boulevard was done in Chinese decor. Her Academy Award was kept in the music room surrounded by her collection of antique dolls.

Twice a year Hattie McDaniel gave a big party for which she did nearly all of the cooking. On those occasions gardenias, her favorite flower, were in every room. Both Hedda Hopper and Louella O. Parsons attended, as did dozens of stars and directors.

For her longest-running part, the title role in the *Beulah* series, Hattie's aprons were handmade by her petite housekeeper, Florence.

Both of Hattie McDaniel's brief marriages ended in divorce. "I think her heart was set on her career," recalls a friend. "When she wasn't working Hattie loved nothing better than to go to the races. When she wasn't on a picture she enjoyed playing the numbers."

Paul Adrian 1979

Aimee Semple McPherson

United Press International Photo

Aimee Semple McPherson, America's most famous and controversial woman evangelist, was once presented by her followers with a seventy-five-pound birthday cake in the shape of Angelus Temple, the huge Church she built at 1100 Glendale Boulevard.

Although the Angelus Temple had a parsonage, Mrs. McPherson chose to live instead on an estate behind this gate at 1982 Micheltorena in Silverlake. Aimee described her home there as "a small cottage."

Paul Adrian 1979

Sister Aimee's famous five-week disappearance or "kidnapping," as she called it, resulted in a series of litigations. Mrs. McPherson is with criminal attorney S.S. Hahn (left) and Jerry Giesler, who defended her successfully. The year was 1928 and Giesler was just coming into his own as *the* Hollywood attorney. Hahn, who was his only serious competitor in handling sordid and sensational cases, took his own life in 1957.

"Get me Giesler!" was the cry that went up from almost all Hollywood celebrities who found themselves in trouble with the law. His office was at 9200 Wilshire Boulevard in Hollywood Hills. Giesler took over the building from Leyland Hayward, the legendary talent agent.

Hayward, who eventually became the producer of *Mister Roberts* and *South Pacific* on Broadway, was also the husband of Margaret Sullavan and the father of Brooke Hayward, the author of *Haywire*.

Aimee Semple McPherson died in 1944 and is buried in the "Slumberland" section of Forest Lawn Memorial Park.

Paul Adrian 1979

Paul Adrian 1979

Sal Mineo

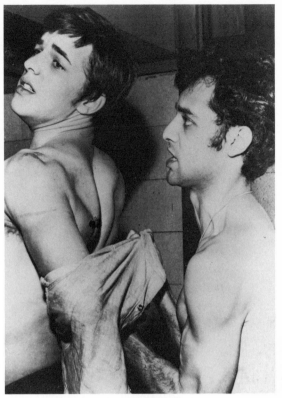

Sal Mineo had just finished making *Rebel Without a Cause* (1955) with James Dean when he posed with bread sticks to demonstrate his drumming skills. Four years later he played the title role in the picture *The Gene Krupa Story*. The following year his part in *Exodus* won him an Academy Award nomination.

By the early seventies Mineo was starring in *Fortune in Men's Eyes,* which he also directed. This still is from the play's Hollywood production at the Coronet Theatre on La Cienega Boulevard. His co-star in that production was Don Johnson.

Sal was in rehearsals for another play when he was stabbed to death on February 12, 1976, in the driveway a few yards to the right of 8563 Holloway Drive in West Hollywood. He lived at 8565 Holloway Drive. He was thirty-seven years old.

Paul Adrian 1980

The Robert Mitchum— Lila Leeds Case

Robert Mitchum and starlet Lila Leeds hardly knew each other when they were handcuffed by police officers and led down the steps on the right at 8443 Ridpath Drive in Laurel Canyon—the "Reefer Roost," as the press called it. They had met for the first time at a party in Marion Davies' Ocean House. They were brought together for the second time by two mutual acquaintances at Lila's rented house in the Hollywood Hills. The date was September 1, 1948, and from then on their names would be linked in one of Hollywood's most publicized scandals.

Robert and Lila were charged with "possession and use of narcotics." The "narcotics" they were caught with were a few marijuana cigarettes, but in 1948 such behavior was viewed by the courts and general public as a serious offense. Their names and faces were smeared across front pages all over the nation and they were each sentenced to a fifty-day jail term.

Ironically, the arrest was a big boost to Mitchum's career. His studio, RKO, rushed his three recently completed movies into release. His "bad boy" image helped them at the box office. Lila Leeds was on the wrong side of Hollywood's double standard. Warner Bros., which had her under contract, dropped her immediately. The only part she could get after that was in an exploitation cheapie, *Wild Weed* (1949).

Tom Mix

Tom Mix, like most of the silent movie people, frequented Musso & Franks Grill. But when Mary Pickford and Claire Windsor went there on Sunday mornings they preferred to have their flannel cakes at a table in the back, away from the windows. Mix liked to sit so passersby could see him.

"He'd wave at them," recalled Viola Dana, "and if they wanted his autograph he'd motion for them to come inside. Tom was a very likable big ham."

Bison Archives

The Musso & Franks Grill has been at its original location (6667 Hollywood Blvd.) since 1919.

Tom Mix lived in a series of homes around the city before moving into his mansion at 1024 Summit Drive in Beverly Hills. His horse, Tony, was kept on the property.

The house was eventually purchased by the architect William Beckett, who completely renovated it.

Western star Tom Mix is standing alongside the car in this photograph, which was taken about 1921. The Mix movies were made mostly at Mixville at 2450 Teviot Street, part of a ranch owned by his producer, William Fox.

A housing project has since been built on the property.

Bison Archives

Marilyn Monroe

Marilyn Monroe was nine years old on September 13, 1935, when she was admitted to the Los Angeles Orphans' Home. One account says that she was pulled into the building screaming, "I'm not an orphan!" But her only parent, her mother, had been committed to a home for the mentally disturbed, and Marilyn, whose name was Norma Jean Baker, remained in the orphanage for twenty-one months.

The institution is now called Hollygrove and is located at 815 El Centro Avenue in Hollywood.

Marilyn Monroe was a stripper at the Mayan Theatre at 1044 South Hill Street in downtown Los Angeles in September 1948. The Mayan was then a rather high-class burlesque house which featured foreign films on its screen.

At first she was billed as Marilyn Monroe, but she became concerned that it would harm the movie career she dreamed of. She changed to Marilyn Marlowe for a few days, and by the time she left after two weeks she was being called Mona Monroe.

Paul Adrian 1979

Paul Adrian 1979

87

The Hollywood Studio Club was designed by Julia Morgan, the chief architect of William Randolph Hearst's San Simeon. Since 1926 it has been a home for young women who moved from all over the nation to Hollywood.

Some of those who came to the movie capital, stayed at the Studio Club and "made it" are Linda Darnell, Donna Reed, Evelyn Keyes, Janet Blair, Gale Storm, Florence Henderson, Dorothy Malone, Barbara Eden and Kim Novak. Ayn Rand wrote *The Night of January 16th* while living in the three-story Mediterranean building at 1215 Lodi Place in Hollywood.

Marilyn Monroe moved into the Studio Club on June 3, 1948. Her rent for room 307, which she shared with another young woman, was $12 a week. Later she lived in room 334 by herself.

On June 19, 1942, just three weeks after her sixteenth birthday, Marilyn Monroe married an eighteen-year-old aircraft worker named Jim Dougherty. Their wedding took place at 432 South Bentley in West Los Angeles.

The couple spent their wedding night and the first few months of their marriage in a one-room apartment with a Murphy bed at 4524 Vista Del Monte in Van Nuys.

Marilyn Monroe was living by herself in an apartment at 882 North Doheny in West Hollywood when she met Joe DiMaggio.

She was almost two hours late for their blind date, dinner at a restaurant on the Sunset Strip. At the time it was called the Villa Nova. (It was also at the Villa Nova that Vincente Minnelli proposed to Judy Garland.) It is now known as the Rainbow Bar and Grill at 9015 Sunset Boulevard.

Marilyn and DiMaggio were married at San Francisco's City Hall and then drove down the Pacific Coast Highway. They spent their wedding night at 125 Spring in Paso Robles. Now an apartment house, it was then called the Clifton Motel.

The DiMaggios lived in the Tudor cottage at 508 North Palm Drive in Beverly Hills until they were divorced.

Marilyn Monroe and Joe DiMaggio had been divorced for only nine days when Joe hired a private detective to break into the apartment at 8122 Waring Avenue in West Hollywood. DiMaggio believed Marilyn was sleeping there with another man. The detective broke into the door on the north side of the building, thinking it was the back door of Marilyn's apartment. The building, however, is a triplex and the apartment he broke into was occupied by a woman who knew nothing of the situation. She was sound asleep and screamed for the police.

Frank Sinatra, who was with DiMaggio on that night in November 1954, was also named in the legal action brought by the woman at 8122 Waring. A sizable settlement was made out of court.

Marilyn was staying with a girlfriend on the west side of the building in an apartment at 754 Kilkea.

Paul Adrian 1979

Paul Adrian 1979

Paul Adrian 1979

Paul Adrian 1979

Paul Adrian 1979

Paul Adrian 1979

Marilyn Monroe's life came to an end in the house she rented at the end of a dead-end street in Brentwood. She lived there with her housekeeper and little dog, Maf, behind a high wall. She was found in the early hours of Sunday, August 5, 1962. Her death was officially listed as "barbiturate overdose."

Marilyn is buried in Westwood Memorial Park in Westwood Village behind the Avco Center Cinemas at 10840 Wilshire Boulevard. The fresh flowers at her tomb are sent regularly by Joe DiMaggio.

Daily News

★★★★ FINAL
DAILY NEWS
NEW YORK'S PICTURE NEWSPAPER®
5¢

MARILYN DEAD

Marilyn Monroe: "I was never used to being happy."

THE MONROE SAGA: 7 PAGES OF STORIES AND PICTURES

MARILYN MONROE
1926 – 1962

Paul Adrian 1979

Montmartre Café

Brandstatter's Montmartre Café was Hollywood's most popular ballroom for many years. The motion picture elite came there in droves from the Roaring Twenties right through the Depression. During Prohibition a patron had to know his waiter well to get a shot of bootleg gin served in a teacup.

The Montmartre was famous for its Saturday-afternoon tea dances and its Charleston contests, which Joan Crawford often won. Gloria Swanson was a regular, as was Dorothy Revier, "the Queen of Poverty Row," who used to punish the parquet with her boyfriend Harry Cohn, the head of Columbia Pictures. Bing Crosby met Dixie Lee, his first wife, at the Montmartre during his engagement there in 1929. When Hoot Gibson took Sally Rand dancing the Montmartre was where they went.

The building that housed Brandstatter's Montmartre Café is at 6763 Hollywood Boulevard near Highland Avenue.

Paul Adrian 1979

Alexander Pantages

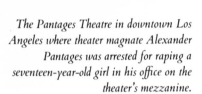

The Pantages Theatre in downtown Los Angeles where theater magnate Alexander Pantages was arrested for raping a seventeen-year-old girl in his office on the theater's mezzanine.

Before the gold-domed building at Seventh and Hill streets in downtown Los Angeles became a jewelry mart it was the Pantages Theatre. The Pantages was a variety house which featured such vaudeville headliners as the Dolly Sisters, Jack Dempsey and Eva Tanguay (the "I Don't Care" girl) and first-run films on its screen.

Alexander Pantages, the illiterate Greek immigrant who owned the largest theater chain in the United States, built an equally sumptuous Pantages Theatre in Hollywood. But when it opened in 1930 its owner was in prison. He had been sentenced to a fifty-year jail term for raping a seventeen-year-old girl in the mezzanine office of the downtown Pantages.

Eventually an appeals court granted Pantages a new trial, at which for the first time in California history evidence of a rape victim's prior sexual conduct was heard in court.

New law was made in that trial, and Pantages was acquitted. The young attorney who brought it all about in his first big case was Jerry Giesler.

The downtown Pantages Theatre is now a jewelry mart.

Bison Archives

The lobby of the Pantages Theatre in Hollywood in 1930.

The Pantages Theatre in Hollywood is at 6233 Hollywood Boulevard near Vine Street. When it opened for the first time with Marion Davies in The Floradora Girl (1930) its owner was serving a prison sentence.
The Oscars were given out at this theater for eleven consecutive years, beginning with those for the year 1949.

Paul Adrian 1979

Dorothy Parker

Dorothy Parker once said that Hollywood was to her a very long, black limousine transporting an exquisitely dressed woman who was taking a large bite out of a bagel.

Mrs. Parker made her reputation at the Algonquin Hotel's Round Table in New York, but for many years she and her husband Alan Campbell lived in Hollywood. Together they worked on such screenplays as *Sweethearts* (1938) and *Trade Winds* (1938). For their scenario of *A Star Is Born* (1937) they were nominated for an Oscar.

In 1937 the couple lived at 602 North Bedford Drive in Beverly Hills. Their last home was at 8983 Norma Place in West Hollywood. It was there that Dorothy Parker found Alan Campbell dead on June 14, 1963.

Dorothy Parker's home at 8983 Norma Place in Hollywood.

Paul Adrian 1979

Mary Pickford, Douglas Fairbanks, Sr., and Buddy Rogers

During her early days in Los Angeles, Mary Pickford lived with her mother in the mansion at 56 Fremont Place, a private road off Wilshire Boulevard.

Mary and her first husband, Owen Moore, lived at 49 Mayberry Road overlooking the Santa Monica Canyon and the Pacific Ocean. The couple were married from 1911 to 1920.

Douglas Fairbanks, Sr., died at age fifty-six in 1939. His widow was the former Lady Sylvia Ashley.

The Fairbanks tomb and reflecting pool are

Sandy Brown Wyeth 1979

An aerial view of Pickfair in 1932.

Pickfair in the late twenties. It was later modernized.

beside the Cathedral Mausoleum in Hollywood Memorial Park Cemetery.

When Buddy Rogers posed for this photograph in 1930 he had made *My Best Girl* (1927) with Mary Pickford, but he was still single and she was still married to Douglas Fairbanks, Sr.

He is standing alongside his DuPont roadster, which cost $5,000. The house in the background was his, at 704 North Bedford Drive in Beverly Hills.

When Douglas Fairbanks, Sr., was courting Mary Pickford, he lived at 1100 Carolyn Way. Around the corner was a hunting lodge set on fifteen acres of Beverly Hills. Fairbanks bought it for $38,000, remodeled it and gave it as a wedding present to his bride, "America's Sweetheart," in 1920. The press immediately dubbed it Pickfair.

The King and Queen of Hollywood reigned from their twenty-two-room mansion until their divorce in 1935. Rudolph Valentino, Pavlova, George Bernard Shaw, Albert Einstein, Greta Garbo and President Calvin Coolidge were some of those who attended the parties at Pickfair. The houseguests included King Umberto of Italy, Lord and Lady Mountbatten and the King and Queen of Siam. "Pickfair," declared *Life Magazine*, "is only slightly less important than the White House ... and much more fun."

A canoe was kept in Pickfair's hundred-foot swimming pool beside an artificial beach. In the lower level of the house was the "Gold Rush Saloon," the walls of which were decorated in Frederic Remington paintings. Rodin drawings, jade carvings and a hundred-piece china set inscribed "Napoléon à Joséphine" were among the other treasures housed at Pickfair.

The third marriage of "America's Sweetheart" was to Buddy Rogers, "America's Boyfriend." It took place at Pickfair in 1937. After her death in 1979 at the age of eighty-six, Rogers placed the property on the market at $10 million. He had attempted to donate it to a university or hospital but none could afford its annual upkeep of over $200,000. It is located at 1143 Summit Drive.

The driveway leading to Pickfair's entryway.

The portico and front door of Pickfair.

The library at Pickfair.

A sitting room at Pickfair.

Marie Prevost

The former Mack Sennett girl had excelled in silents as both a comedienne and a dramatic actress. During the twenties she was married to prominent leading man Kenneth Harlan. But talking pictures had slowed her career to a standstill. By 1937 Marie was glad to take the few bit parts that were offered to her.

Marie Prevost had been dead two days before she was found in her apartment at 6230 Afton Place in Hollywood. Her sole companion, a dachshund named Maxie, was by her side whining. Tiny tooth marks, made when her pet had tried in vain to wake her, were visible on her arm.

There were several empty whiskey bottles near the sink and notices from her bank that some of her checks had been returned marked "insufficient funds."

The only evidence of contact with her former life was the duplicate of a promissory note for a loan made to her shortly before her death. It was signed "Joan Crawford."

Paul Adrian 1979

George Reeves

Fans of the *Superman* television series will recognize this as the *Daily Planet* building where "Clark Kent" and "Lois Lane" worked as reporters. It is located downtown at 200 North Spring Street and is the Los Angeles City Hall.

Entrances and exits to the *Daily Planet* building were filmed at the Carnation Building at 5045 Wilshire Blvd.

George Reeves, who played the title role on the program, was upset because he had become so closely identified with the part of "Superman." He was afraid that playing the Man of Steel for so long had already typecast him.

Reeves was found dead in his home at 1579 Benedict Canyon Road in Beverly Hills in the early hours of June 16, 1959. He was naked and had been shot through the head by a .30 caliber Luger. The cause of death was listed officially as "suicide," something that neither his mother nor several of his close friends ever believed.

Paul Adrian 1979

Wallace Reid

Wallace Reid was one of the most popular movie stars in the world when he went on location to make *The Valley of the Giants* (1919). During the filming he injured his back and was given daily doses of morphine to relieve the pain. After three months of continued use he was addicted. As his good looks began to deteriorate he took to heavy drinking as well. By 1922 Reid had the wasted appearance of what was then called a "dope fiend."

He entered a sanitarium at 5227 Santa Monica Boulevard, where he died on January 18, 1923. Ten thousand fans and friends attended his funeral. He was thirty-one years old.

Residence of Wallace Reid, Hollywood, California.

This old postcard shows the house that Wallace Reid built in 1920 for $23,000. It stood on the corner of Sweetzer and DeLongpre. The back of the Reid home was on Sunset Boulevard, which was not yet a paved street. The swimming pool at the right was the first ever in Hollywood. Ruth Roland, the serial star, had a home just a block away at 1466 North Sweetzer.

A hotel-apartment house now fills the entire corner.

Western star William S. Hart lived next door to Wallace Reid at 1581 DeLongpre. His home is now occupied by The Actors Studio.

Paul Adrian 1979

Tommy Rettig

One evening in the late summer of 1959 a fifteen-year-old girl named Darlene was sitting on the bus bench on the northwest corner of Sunset Boulevard and La Brea. Darlene never missed the *Lassie* show on television. She had a big crush on its star, Tommy Rettig. He was her "absolute ideal."

When two boys pulled up in a car and offered Darlene and her friend a ride, she said no automatically. As they drove away her friend told Darlene she thought that one of the boys was Tommy Rettig. Darlene "just about died." A few minutes later the car returned and she got a good look at the boy. It was Tommy Rettig.

The two young men seated on that same bus bench in 1979 are (left to right) Tom, Jr., and Deane Rettig, the sons of Tommy and Darlene Rettig.

Tommy Rettig, Sr., 1979

Lili St. Cyr

Lili St. Cyr was the world's most famous artist of striptease when she retired in 1964. She had risen from headliner on the burlesque wheels to star in nightclubs and movies.

In 1951 Lili was arrested for lewdness during her engagement at Ciro's. Jerry Giesler charged her $2,000 to turn the charges into a joke in the courtroom.

When she was making as much as $7,500 weekly her most famous act was Lili as a little girl who, arising in the morning, slips out of her nightie and into a bathtub. The tub had a glass front and a lot of bubbles—but not too many. Afterward she would get dressed in front of her audience. No performer ever appealed more to fetishists than Lili St. Cyr.

Former fans and those who know of her only by reputation drop by or send in orders to the Undie World of Lili St. Cyr at 8104 Santa Monica Boulevard in West Hollywood. The shop offers for sale the same type of highly abbreviated undergarments she wore on stage. The sign outside gives the "ecdysiast" top billing. Beneath her famous name is the merchandise being offered—"lingerie and provocatives."

Paul Adrian 1979

Sundays at Salka's

Greta Garbo used to come by the Viertel home often. She and Salka frequently took walks together along the beach nearby.

Photo courtesy of Peter Viertel

The unpretentious house at 165 Mayberry Road in Santa Monica was from the early thirties right into the fifties the gathering place of the European intellectual-artistic colony in Hollywood. Names that did much to shape the twentieth century came there as they would have to their favorite café in their homelands. Such was the ambiance of the house of Salka Viertel.

Salka had worked in Europe as both a writer and actress with the legendary Max Reinhardt. She came to Hollywood with her husband, Berthold Viertel, who was collaborating with the director F. W. Murnau. She remained for over two decades, during which time she became M-G-M's "Garbo specialist." Salka received screen credit as co-author of Garbo's vehicles *Queen Christina* and *Conquest*.

During World War II, 165 Mayberry Road was a great refuge for those fleeing Nazi persecution. Later the Viertels helped the victims of the blacklist of the McCarthy era.

The Viertels entertained often, but Sundays were considered open house. Hearty, stimulating conversation and the chance of meeting other world figures drew Sergei Eisenstein, Arnold Schoenberg, Harold Clurman, George Cukor and Charles Chaplin there regularly. Salka's soirées offered an opportunity for a complete unknown such as Fred Zinneman to sit and talk with an established director like William Dieterle or the star Paul Muni. It was there that Christopher Isherwood first met Bertolt Brecht, whose lover, Ruth Berlau, lived over the Viertel garage.

Thomas Mann visited the Mayberry Road house frequently. When his brother Heinrich's seventieth birthday was celebrated there both Manns hosted a party that included Leon Feuchtwanger, Alfred Doblin and Franz Werfel. Igor Stravinsky and Aldous Huxley were regulars.

Paul Adrian

The Viertel house at 165 Mayberry Road in Santa Monica.

Greta Garbo lived for a while in the thirties in a house she rented at 1717 San Vicente Boulevard. It was a short walk to 165 Mayberry Road.

Paul Adrian

Samson's Salon

Samson DeBrier in his salon, which Esquire *magazine once described as "a gentle junkyard, a repository of rotting portiers, chipped gilt frames, Regency ball gowns on wooden dress dummies, disintegrating first editions stacked on floors, tables and love seats; of dusty whorehouse mirrors; of gold-plated peacocks with zircon wings. . . ."*

The three houses which form the compound at 6026 Barton, just off Vine Street in Hollywood, were for years the settings of nightly gatherings of Hollywood's celebrated, up and coming and down and out. About ten o'clock each evening people began to arrive. Often it was dawn before the last guest left. Neither food nor drink was ever served. No invitations were given. All were welcome as long as they behaved in a civilized manner and especially if they were good talkers and/or good listeners.

Unknowns such as Sally Kellerman, Louise Fletcher and Jack Nicholson mingled with the likes of Marlon Brando, Tony Richardson and Dorothy Parker. Richard Burton was a regular, as were Stanley Kubrick and Anaïs Nin. Steve McQueen, Tennessee Williams and Jack Lemmon came. So did "Spivy" and Dody Goodman. Rod McKuen, Dean Stockwell, "Vampira," Diane Varsi and James Dean made up the younger set.

The soirées were presided over by Samson DeBrier, the son of a Russian mother and a Rumanian father. Born in China in 1904, DeBrier was raised in Atlantic City, New Jersey. He left the United States in the late twenties for Paris, where he immediately entered into an affair with André Gide. After being taken to tea at the home of Gertrude Stein, DeBrier wrote in his journal: "I have just met the famous Gertrude Stein. I didn't like her very much."

Samson came to Hollywood in 1942

and worked for years in the psychiatric ward of the Veterans Hospital, where he looked after patients who were being subjected to shock therapy.

Always at ease with the creative, the eccentric and the notorious, DeBrier was the close friend of Evelyn Nesbit, "the Girl in the Red Velvet Swing." Her multimillionaire husband Harry K. Thaw shot and killed architect Stanford White on the roof garden of Madison Square Garden. It was called at the time, 1906, "the Crime of the Century." Another of his friends was the illegitimate daughter of Al Capone.

After Samson ended his salon in 1967 he became as well known as a guest as he had been as a host. Many stars felt their parties were incomplete without him. Producers and directors believed his presence brought them luck at screenings. Having DeBrier at one's table added a certain cachet to any Hollywood dinner party. Personalities such as Warren Beatty and Paul Mazursky took him to dinner in smart restaurants. He could be seen at the Cannes Film Festival seated with Charlie Chaplin.

But DeBrier was considered by some to be something more than a great catalyst. Many claimed that he was a witch. He was quoted as saying that when he was twelve years old he'd discovered that he had "certain powers." Whenever asked directly if he was in fact a warlock he replied: "I always think of myself as just an All-American boy."

Paul Adrian

The main house at 6026 Barton was built around 1910. Kenneth Anger's film The Inauguration of the Pleasure Dome *(1956) was filmed there. Elaine May was supporting herself by selling aluminum siding from door to door when she was one of DeBrier's tenants in 1952.*

Evelyn Nesbit, "the Girl in the Red Velvet Swing," in 1904, two years before she became involved in "the Crime of the Century."

Evelyn Nesbit is buried in Holy Cross Cemetery near the Los Angeles International Airport.

MOTHER
EVELYN FLORENCE NESBIT
1884 ✝ 1967

Paul Adrian

Gloria Swanson

The house Gloria Swanson lived in as "Norma Desmond" in *Sunset Boulevard* (1950) was at the southwest corner of Wilshire Boulevard and Irving in Los Angeles. The swimming pool William Holden as "Joe Gillis" ended up floating in was built for the picture. Because of zoning in that area it had to be removed later at studio expense. When *Sunset Boulevard* was made there the house had not been lived in for over twenty years and was referred to locally as the "Ghost Mansion." The movie *Rebel Without a Cause* (1950) also used it as a location.

In 1957 the owner of the "Ghost Mansion," billionaire J. Paul Getty, had the house torn down and replaced by an office building.

William Holden played the unemployed screenwriter "Joe Gillis" in *Sunset Boulevard*. He tells the audience in the early part of the picture that he is living "temporarily" at the Alto Nido Apartments. That building is at 1851 North Ivar at the corner of Franklin. It can be seen from the Hollywood Freeway.

Paul Adr

The gated entryway to the Paramount studios through which Gloria Swanson was chauffeured in an Isotta-Fraschini in *Sunset Boulevard* can be seen from the corner of Melrose and Bronson in Hollywood.

In the movie the automobile was supposed to be driven by Erich von Stroheim, who played her manservant (as well as former husband and director), "Max von Mayerling."

In fact von Stroheim could not drive. A cable was tied to the front bumper and the car was pulled onto the movie lot.

The original Brown Derby restaurant was inherited by Gloria Swanson's daughter from her father, Herbert K. Somborn, who founded the restaurant in 1926. There is also a Brown Derby at 1628 North Vine Street in Hollywood and another at 9537 Wilshire Boulevard in Beverly Hills. But the original was located at 3377 Wilshire Boulevard, directly across the street from the Ambassador Hotel.

It is in the original Brown Derby that the famous Cobb Salad was created by its manager, Bob Cobb. It came about when Cobb's wife, movie actress Gail Patrick, told him that she wished vegetables in salads would be chopped very fine.

In Hollywood's heyday, Louella O. Parsons always sat in the Derby's booth number two. Hedda Hopper, her archrival as a movie gossip columnist, was across the aisle in number five. Some say that Clark Gable proposed to Carole Lombard in booth number seven. At least that was where they always sat together.

The original Brown Derby in 1930.

Paul Adrian 1979

The Brown Derby 1979.

Paul Adrian 1979

Rudolph Valentino, John Barrymore, and F. Scott and Zelda Fitzgerald lived at one time or another in the palatial Siesta Cottage on the grounds of the Ambassador Hotel.

Gloria Swanson lived there with her second husband, Herbert K. Somborn, whose family owned the Ambassador, which is at 3400 Wilshire Boulevard in Los Angeles.

The Ambassador is now owned by the family of G. David Schine, the central figure in the famed Army-McCarthy hearing of the early fifties.

The Ambassador is the home of the famous Coconut Grove nightclub. It was in the pantry of the hotel that Bobby Kennedy was assassinated.

In the Ambassador Hotel's Coconut Grove, Bing Crosby had his first big success crooning with Paul Whiteman's orchestra. It is also where Bing proposed to his first wife, Dixie Lee.

The Academy Awards ceremony was held at the Coconut Grove for six years. In this photograph, which was taken on November 18, 1932, Louis B. Mayer of M-G-M is presenting Helen Hayes with the Oscar for her performance in *The Sin of Madelon Claudet.* Lionel Barrymore is seated at right.

William Desmond Taylor

In 1922 Paramount Pictures was still located on the northeast corner of Sunset Boulevard and Vine Street. The handsome William Desmond Taylor was one of the studio's most prominent directors. He was also considered to be one of Hollywood's most eligible bachelors. It wasn't until he was found murdered that the world learned he had deserted his wife and daughter and changed his name before coming to Hollywood.

Taylor was found shot to death on the first floor of the duplex he occupied at 404½ South Alvarado Street on the morning of February 2, 1922. Edna Purviance, Chaplin's leading lady and intimate friend, lived in the other half of the murder building. A supermarket replaced all of the apartments in 1965.

Bison Archives

Art Ronnie

Paul Adrian 1979

109

The investigation of the Taylor murder, which has never been solved, brought rumors of drug trafficking and homosexuality. The bad publicity received by Mabel Normand, who was the last person known to have seen the director alive, cast a pall over the screen comedienne's career.

Ethereal Mary Miles Minter was called "the Golden Girl of the Screen." Paramount Pictures publicized her as virginal. Her studio hoped she would become as popular as Mary Pickford. That image and hope were shattered forever when the teenage beauty arrived at the murder scene and declared her undying love for Taylor in a hysterical outburst. Crowds and police witnessed what one newspaper described as "her greatest performance." Then her love letters to the director were found in one of his boots and a couple of pink silk nightgowns monogrammed "M.M.M." were discovered in his bedroom.

Paramount paid Mary Miles Minter $350,000 to dissolve her contract the following year.

Although she was never charged with the crime, Charlotte Shelby, the domineering mother of Mary Miles Minter, was a prime suspect in the case. Mrs. Shelby died in 1957 at 144 Adelaide Drive in Santa Monica. In 1981 Mary Miles Minter was still living there in seclusion.

The remains of the murdered director William Desmond Taylor are marked William C. Deane-Tanner, the name he dropped when he vanished from New York City in 1908. His tomb in the Cathedral Mausoleum of Hollywood Memorial Park Cemetery was paid for by the daughter whom he had deserted years before.

IN MEMORY OF
WILLIAM C. DEANE-TANNER
BELOVED FATHER OF
ETHEL D. DEANE-TANNER
DIED FEBRUARY 1 1922

Shirley Temple

Paul Adrian 1979

Fans imagined a precious little cottage. In fact the "doll house" was called that only because it housed Shirley's large collection of dolls in glass cases. It also had room for two garages, a maid's quarters and Shirley's much-photographed soda fountain. There was a bomb shelter in the basement and a walk-in vault. The living room of the "doll house" could accommodate a couch which was twenty feet long.

Mr. and Mrs. Temple had two sons when their only daughter was born on April 23, 1928. The child star who was to top the popularity polls for several years during the thirties was born in Santa Monica Hospital.

Shirley's first home was the two-bedroom bungalow at 948 24th Street in Santa Monica.

When Shirley Temple and John Agar were married at the Wilshire Methodist Church in 1945 they were the most admired and envied newlyweds in the country.

The publicists for the Agars told the world that Shirley and her new husband (and soon-to-be movie star) would live on his earnings. Hers would be saved for their future. One of their economies was that they would make their home in Shirley's doll house, which was behind her parents' mansion at 227 North Rockingham in Brentwood.

Paul Adrian 1980

Thelma Todd

Thelma Todd was a grammar school teacher before Jesse Lasky brought her to Hollywood, where she became the "Ice Cream Blonde" of the movies. Both beautiful and lively, she developed quite a following from her appearances in pictures with the Marx brothers and Laurel and Hardy.

On the evening of December 15, 1935, Ida Lupino gave a party for Thelma at the Café Trocadero, the smartest nightclub on the Sunset Strip. The next morning she was found wearing her blue-and-silver evening gown, a mink coat and quite a few diamonds. Thelma was dead of carbon monoxide poisoning. She lived above her restaurant, Thelma Todd's Sidewalk Café, a high-priced, popular hangout for movie stars at the beach.

Thelma had been chauffeured home after the party and had walked up the one hundred stairs leading to her apartment in high heels. She was found in the garage inside her chocolate Lincoln Phaeton.

There were many clues and contradictory stories, and even some whispers about gambling and drug traffic. Lucky Luciano was one of the names mentioned in connection with her death. The case is unsolved, but in 1976 Pat Di Cicco, the once-powerful agent and the former husband of Thelma Todd, said that he had long believed that Roland West, who had been her partner in the restaurant, was responsible for her death.

The Café Trocadero opened on September 15, 1934, and continued in operation until 1946. This photograph was taken in 1937 when Adrian had an interior-decorating studio at the far left of this picture. The Pierce Arrow convertible parked outside belonged to Adrian's secretary.

On December 16, 1935, the body of Thelma Todd was found in this garage at 17531 Posetano Road in Pacific Palisades.

The three steps which once led to the Café Trocadero can still be seen at 8610 Sunset Boulevard at the corner of Sunset Plaza Drive. The building to the left was built in 1938 for Adrian, who had his salon there for a number of years.

The property that housed Thelma Todd's Sidewalk Café and apartment is at 17575 Pacific Coast Highway. It faces the Pacific Ocean. It was left to Lola Lane, the senior of the Lane sisters of movies, by her husband, director-writer Roland West. It is now used by the Paulist Fathers as a production center for their TV films.

The Tone-Payton-Neal Triangle

Franchot Tone often lost the girl to another man in his movies. In real life he didn't take it so well.

Tone was very much in love with a voluptuous twenty-five-year-old blonde, Barbara Payton, and he had told people that they were going to be married. When he learned Barbara had also been seeing movie tough guy Tom Neal, Tone was enraged.

The triangle finally came together in the walled courtyard of Barbara Payton's apartment at 1803 Courtney Terrace in Hollywood. The time was 2:00 A.M. on September 14, 1951. Neal, age thirty-seven, who had been a Golden Gloves contender, sent Tone, age forty-six, to the hospital with a concussion and a broken nose.

Paul Adrian 1979

The Turnabout Theatre

The Yale Puppeteers were known in Hollywood from 1930, when they brought their traveling show to Olvera Street in downtown Los Angeles for a two-year stand. In 1934 they supported Lillian Harvey in her movie *I Am Suzanne*.

On July 10, 1941, the Turnabout Theatre opened at 716 La Cienega Boulevard, where they played six nights a week for the next fifteen years.

The puppet show was the first half of the evening. At intermission coffee was served in the patio. Then the small band would play "Turn About, Turn About, Turn Your Troubles Inside Out" as the audience would turn the 180 streetcar seats around to face another stage. There Elsa Lanchester, who was there for twelve years, or Lotte Goslar, who was there for ten years, would perform special material. Dorothy Neumann and Leota Lane, the Lane sister who didn't go into the movies, were others who contributed to the delicious nonsense.

Guest stars for the second half were Marais and Miranda, the Duncan sisters, Gilda Gray ("the Queen of Shimmy"), El Brendel and Virginia O'Brien.

The shows changed many times during the years, but the appeal was always a sophisticated one—a combination of political and social satire, what would then have been considered "risqué" and what would now be called "high camp."

Time magazine summed it all up as "Hollywood's toniest vaudeville show."

The patio and entrance to the Turnabout Theatre at 716 North Cienega Boulevard.

From left to right: Dorothy Neumann, Harry Burnett, Frances Osborne, Elsa Lanchester, Forman Brown, Lotte Goslar.

Lana Turner

Judy Turner did not like her typing class at Hollywood High School. Several times she had broken one of her long, pretty fingernails on the keyboard. One afternoon in January 1936, she cut typing class and went instead across the street to the northeast corner of Highland Avenue and Sunset Boulevard, where there was a malt shop.

Billy Wilkerson, owner of the *Hollywood Reporter* and the Trocadero, saw the auburn-haired girl sitting at the counter sipping a Coke. He asked her if she would like to be in movies.

"I don't know," replied the sixteen-year-old. "I'll have to ask my mother."

Judy was signed to a contract by Metro-Goldwyn-Mayer. The studio changed her name to Lana Turner, bleached her hair blond and called her "the Sweater Girl." After playing supporting parts in *They Won't Forget* (1937) and *Love Finds Andy Hardy* (1939) she became one of M-G-M's hottest properties.

A service station now stands on the corner where Lana Turner was discovered.

Paul Adrian 1979   Paul Adrian 1979

Lana Turner was starred by M-G-M in such pictures as *Honky Tonk* (1941) with Clark Gable, *The Postman Always Rings Twice* (1946) with John Garfield and *The Bad and the Beautiful* (1952). She married and divorced band leader Artie Shaw, millionaire-playboy Bob Topping, actor Lex Barker and restaurateur Stephen Crane, the father of her only child.

On April 5, 1958, Beverly Hills police were called to the home of Lana Turner, on North Bedford Drive. When they arrived the door was opened by criminal lawyer Jerry Giesler, who led them upstairs to the star's all-pink bedroom. Lying on the floor in a pool of blood was the body of Lana's lover, small-time hoodlum Johnny Stompanato. He had been stabbed to death with a butcher knife by Lana's fifteen-year-old daughter, Cheryl Crane.

Merv Griffin has subsequently lived in this house.

Paul Adrian 1979

Rudolph Valentino

Valentino kept an apartment in the building at 716 Valentino Place next to Paramount Pictures in Hollywood. It is there he entertained Jean Acker, who became his first wife.

Another place he stayed from time to time was the Hollywood Athletic Club at 6525 Sunset Boulevard, now an office building. The "HAC" can still be seen over the doorway.

Natacha Rambova lived in a cottage at 6612 Sunset Boulevard until she and Valentino were married in 1922. The couple spent a great deal of time there, working in the garden that was then behind the house and applying lacquer to the Chinese furniture that they both liked.

Although it was long ago converted into shops, the building is still there.

Paul Adrian 1979

6525

6612   photo king l

466-2977

Paul Adrian 1979

Paul Adrian 1979

In 1924 Rudolph Valentino bought Falcon Lair, a thirteen-room mansion on over seven acres of Beverly Hills, for $150,000. During the Depression when the property was put up for auction there was only one bidder. Falcon Lair went at that time for $18,000.

As late as the mid-forties Ann Harding was able to purchase the estate for $80,000.

Billionairess Doris Duke was another of its owner-residents.

The words "Falcon Lair" can be seen at the top of the pillars on either side of the gates at 1436 Bella Drive.

Paul Adrian 1979

Paul Adrian 1979

Valentino at the stables of Falcon Lair, which are below the main house at 10051 Cielo Drive. It is in front of this building, now a residence, that Ingrid Bergman and Roberto Rossellini used to meet secretly before the world knew of their relationship.

Michael Back

This Brunswick phonograph belonged to Rudolph Valentino. It was in Falcon Lair when he died.

119

Rudolph Valentino is posed beside his new Voisin in front of his house in 1924. The building, which was at 6776 Wedgewood Place in the Whitley Heights area of Hollywood, was demolished in 1951 to make way for the Hollywood Freeway. The foundation of the home can still be seen from the Highland Avenue exit of the freeway.

Valentino lived in this house from 1922 until 1924.

In 1935 the two-story house, which was on one acre of land, was sold for $5,000.

While in Paris on his honeymoon in 1923 with his second wife, Natacha Rambova, Valentino ordered this four-cylinder, sleeve-valved Voisin Sporting Victoria. It was delivered in 1924 and cost $14,000.

The cobra hood ornament was his personal symbol and appeared on many of Valentino's possessions.

The automobile is on display at the Merle Norman Cosmetics Tower of Beauty in Sylmar, California.

Rudolph Valentino owned over a dozen dogs, but his favorite was Kabar, a black Doberman. After Valentino's death, Kabar was taken by Mauritz Stiller, the director who brought Garbo to prominence in the European cinema.

Kabar survived his master by only three years. "He died," said Valentino's nephew, "of a broken heart."

Kabar is buried at the SPCA Pet Cemetery at 5068 Old Scandia Lane in Calabasas, California.

One of Mary Pickford's dogs is also buried there, as are Topper, Hopalong Cassidy's horse, and Pete, the *Our Gang (Little Rascals)* dog.

Rudolph Valentino is buried in the Cathedral Mausoleum of the Hollywood Memorial Park Cemetery at 6000 Santa Monica Boulevard. It is directly behind Paramount Pictures.

Valentino's crypt is next to the remains of June Mathis, the screenwriter who insisted on him for the lead in *The Four Horsemen of the Apocalypse* (1921). It was that film, which she wrote, that made him a star.

A memorial service is conducted beside his tomb every August 23 at 12:10 P.M., the exact time of his death.

The Valentino Memorial, entitled "Inspiration," is in DeLongpre Park on DeLongpre Avenue in Hollywood. The inscription at its base reads:

Paul Adrian 1979

Erected in Memory of Rudolph Valentino
1895—1926

Presented by his friends and admirers from every walk of life in all parts of the world in appreciation of the happiness brought to them by his cinema portrayals.

A bronze head of the screen's great Latin lover stands beside the memorial.

Lupe Velez and Gary Cooper

Paul Adrian 1979

Lupe Velez, "the Mexican Spitfire," had affairs with John Gilbert and Randolph Scott, but neither of those relationships had the intensity of her romance with Gary Cooper. The two co-starred in *Wolf Song* (1929) and lived together behind the iron gates in the Spanish house at 1826 Laurel Canyon Boulevard in Hollywood until 1931. They would probably have married if it had not been for the strong disapproval of Cooper's parents.

Steven Arnold 1980

Gary Cooper loved cars almost as much as he did women. One of the two Duesenbergs he owned is on display at the Briggs Cunningham Automotive Museum in Costa Mesa, California. Only two of this short-chassis Model SJ were ever made. The other was owned by Clark Gable.

Cooper and Gable took delivery on their Duesenbergs in 1935. They had straight-eight engines, four valves per cylinder and dual carburetors to the supercharger. The bodies were by La Grande.

After Lupe and Gary broke up she was married for six stormy years to Johnny Weissmuller. When they were divorced in 1939, Lupe retained possession of their pink stucco mansion at 732 North Rodeo Drive. It was in that house in Beverly Hills that she died of an overdose of sleeping pills on December 13, 1944. The star was four months pregnant by an unknown actor, several years her junior, whom she referred to as "the one love of my life."

Steven Arnold 1980

Paul Adrian 1979

The Wanger-Bennett-Lang Triangle

Joan Bennett, the younger sister of Constance Bennett, was a blonde on the screen until she made Trade Winds *(1938).*

Producer Walter Wanger and Joan Bennett were married in 1941.

Joan Bennett, the younger sister of Constance Bennett, was a blonde until she donned a black wig for her role in *Trade Winds* (1938). She remained a brunette after that. Joan and the film's producer, Walter Wanger, were married in 1941.

At 5:30 P.M. on December 13, 1951, Joan Bennett was sitting in her 1948 Cadillac convertible, which was parked in the lot on Rexford Drive near Santa Monica Boulevard in Beverly Hills. She was talking with Jennings Lang, her agent at Music Corporation of America, the large white building across the street from where they were. Her husband had warned Lang only a few weeks before that if anyone ever came between him and his wife there would be serious consequences.

Lang was standing alongside Joan's car, leaning on the door. She looked up to see Wanger walking toward them with a gun in his hand.

"Don't, Walter! Don't be silly!" cried Lang as Wanger fired twice. Only one bullet hit Lang—in the groin.

Walter Wanger was arrested. Joan Bennett phoned her press agent and then went into seclusion. She testified in Wanger's behalf in court, where he was represented by Jerry Giesler.

The outcome of it all was that Wanger spent four months on an honor farm. Upon his release he produced the picture *Riot in Cell Block 11* (1954). Joan Bennett and Walter Wanger were still married when he died in 1965.

The building at 9370 Santa Monica Boulevard is now the headquarters of a conglomerate. Music Corporation of America is no longer a talent agency. It owns Universal Pictures, where Jennings Lang works as an executive producer.

The offices of a conglomerate are now housed in the building at 9370 Santa Monica Boulevard. It was once the West Coast headquarters of the giant talent agency MCA.

Nathanael West

Photograph "West in 1931" from *Nathanael West: The Art of His Life* by Jay Martin. Copyright © 1970 by Jay Martin. Reprinted by permission of Farrar, Straus and Giroux, Inc.

In Nathanael West's novel *The Day of the Locust* (1939) the main character, "Todd Hackett," lived in a shabby bungalow court in Hollywood. While West was conceiving this book he lived at the Parva-Sed, an apartment house at 1817 Ivar just above Hollywood Boulevard. He wrote the book, which was made into a movie in 1975, while working as a night clerk at the Sutton East Hotel on Manhattan's East 56th Street.

West had little success in Hollywood, where he worked on and off as a screenwriter of B pictures. When he lived at the Parva-Sed in 1935, many of his neighbors in the building were prostitutes. The writer was intrigued with them and used to drive the women to and from their "dates." They in turn would wash his dishes and sew buttons on his clothes.

Jess Willard

On October 4, 1930, the former world heavyweight boxing champion (1915–19) opened Jess Willard's Food Department Store in Hollywood. A new concept at the time in food retailing, the store housed fifteen different concessions, all of which sold food delicacies. Another unusual aspect of the venture was that Willard's store remained open twenty-four hours every day, seven days a week.

The opening-day theme was a Mexican fiesta with two orchestras, vaudeville acts and movie personalities in person.

The land and building, which still stands on the northeast corner of Afton Place and Vine Street, then cost $330,000.

JESS WILLARD EASY VICT
OVER FRANK MORAN; LO
ONE ROUND ONLY; TWO E

Champion Jabs, Smashes and Upp
Challenger Almost at Will; Hu
Right Hand in Third Inning.

IRISHMAN GAME BUT BADLY BATT

Right Eye Cut, Left Nearly Clos
Blows From Jess' Fists; Nate Ja
son Wins Preliminary.

NEW YORK, March 25.—Jess Willard, champio
weight of the world, easily outpointed Frank Moran
round bout here Saturday night. Willard had the
points in every round except the third, which went
by a narrow margin and the eighth and ninth which w

126

The Witch's House

"The Witch's House" is what many Beverly Hills residents called this structure at Carmelita and Walden Drive.

Originally it was the administration building of the Willat Studios at 6509 West Washington Boulevard in Culver City. It was moved to its present location about forty years ago and has been a private residence ever since.

In the film *The Loved One* it was used as John Gielgud's house.

Wil Wright's

The original Wil Wright's ice cream parlor was at 8641 Sunset Boulevard.

Beginning in May 1946 and for twenty-four years thereafter a small shop on the Sunset Strip served the richest ice cream in America—"24% butterfat"—to the most famous people in the world.

Groucho Marx seemed unable to pass the candy-striped awning without indulging in a sundae or cone. Garbo used to sit at one of the marble-topped tables with her head turned away from the windows. Autograph seekers were always around hoping to catch personalities like Jack Benny, Eleanor Roosevelt, Robert Taylor and Ali Khan.

Behind the counter, wearing candy-striped coats, scooping up such flavors as Pink Grapefruit Ice and Jamaican Ginger, were actors-to-be Tab Hunter, Nick Adams and Leonard Nimoy.

"It's Heavenly" was Wil Wright's motto. "It's addictive" is what customers said about it. Ingrid Bergman had it flown to Europe. So did Elizabeth Taylor. Howard Hughes

sent his trusted executives to pick up quarts of it for him.

When "Amos 'n' Andy" had dinner with their friend President Eisenhower, they brought the dessert with them—Wil Wright's ice cream all the way to the White House.

Natalie Wood helps herself to the freshly whipped cream. Wil Wright is behind her.